THE RULES OF

DOUBLE–ENTRY BOOKKEEPING

PARTICULARIS DE COMPUTIS

ET SCRIPTURIS

LUCA PACIOLI
A.D. 1494

Chair of Mathematics at the
University of Perugia

Professor of Mathematics in the
Sapienza University of Rome

IICPA Publications

The Rules of Double–Entry Bookkeeping.
Particularis de computis et scripturis.

Originally published as the 11th Treatise of Section Nine of the *Summa de arithmetica, geometria, proportioni et proportionalita.* Venice, Italy, A.D. 1494. English translation from John B. Geijsbeek (1914) in "Ancient Double-Entry Bookkeeping". Denver, Colorado, pp. 32-80.

Luca Pacioli, 1445–1515
  The Rules of Double–Entry Bookkeeping. *Particularis de computis et scripturis.*
  108 pages.

ISBN - 10   1453702024
EAN - 13   9781453702024

IICPA Publications,
International Institute of Certified Public Accountants Incorporated

Website: www.iicpa.com

Picture on the front cover:
Pacioli's portrait. Painting by Jacobo de Barbari (1495), Museo Nazionale di Capodimonte. Naples, Italy.

2e 2010-09-22

TABLE OF CONTENTS

FOREWORD BY THE EDITOR

Luca **Bartolomeo de** *Pacioli* (sometimes Paciolo) (1446/7, Sansepolcro −1517) grew up and died in Tuscany, Italy. In 1472 Pacioli took the vows of a Franciscan monk, and in 1475, at about 28 years of age, became the first Chair of Mathematics at the nearby University of Perugia. Later in his influential career, in 1514, Pacioli was appointed by Pope Leo X to Professor of Mathematics in the Sapienza University of Rome, a position of the highest ranking.

Pacioli's historic treatise on double-entry bookkeeping, published in 1494, entitled *"Particularis de computis et scripturis"* ("Details of Computation and Recording"), is probably the first published book on double-entry bookkeeping, a historic document and a bestseller at its time printed on the Gutenberg press, providing a detailed description of the Venetian system of accounting. The treatise is contained in his larger work *"Summa de arithmetica, geometria, proportioni et propor-tionalita"*.[1]

"Pacioli's important manuscript made him instantly famous, and he was invited to Milan to teach mathematics at the Court of Duke Lodovico Maria Sforzo. One of his pupils would be Leonardo da Vinci (1452-1519). During the seven years Pacioli and da Vinci spent together, the two would help each other create two masterpieces that withstood the test of time.

---

[1] "The Gutenberg press, on which my Summa was printed in 1494, had reached Venice only in 1469." (Weis, William L. "Luca Pacioli: Renaissance accountant." *Journal of Accountancy,* Vol. 172, 1991.)

Luca Pacioli taught Leonardo da Vinci the geometry for his mural painting *The Last Supper* (Italian: *Il Cenacolo* or *L'Ultima Cena*) created by da Vinci for his patron, the Duke Ludovico Sforza and his duchess Beatrice d'Este between 1495 and 1498, representing the scene of The Last Supper from the final days of Jesus as narrated in the Gospel of John 13:21, when Jesus announced that one of his Twelve Apostles would betray him.

Da Vinci illustrated Pacioli's next and second most important manuscript *De Divina Proportione* ("Of Divine Proportions") published in 1509. Pacioli taught da Vinci perspective and proportionality. This knowledge allowed da Vinci to create one of his greatest masterpieces, a mural on the north wall of the Santa Maria de Gracia Dominican cloister in Milan measuring 15 feet × 29 feet. This mural is the most famous painting of the fifteenth century, known as "The Last Supper." The geometry Pacioli taught da Vinci would occur in many of da Vinci's later works. Da Vinci mentions Pacioli many times in his notes."[2]

---

[2] "Luca Pacioli: The Father of Accounting." Online at http://flynf.tripod.com/pacioli.htm. Retrieved 2010-07-10.

"It is not at all surprising to find a treatise of mercantile procedures in a book on mathematics. At the time, mercantile arithmetic was an established part of mathematics, and its teachers were mathematicians."[3]

Prior to its first publication in 1494, Pacioli had been working on the *Summa de Arithmetica* for some thirty years. He felt that his teaching had fallen to a low ebb and thought that the shortcoming lay in the use of improper methods and in the scarcity of available literature. Pacioli sought to correct these faults in the *Summa* which is divided into the following parts: 1. Arithmetic and algebra. 2. Their use in trade reckoning. 3. Bookkeeping. 4. Money and exchange. 5. Pure and especially applied geometry.

The 'novelty' of double-entry bookkeeping is that all business transactions are recorded in a systematic self-balancing way consisting of the debit(s) (*dee dare*—shall give) and the credit(s) (*dee avere or havere*—shall have). After the merchant takes his inventory of all of his possessions, and all of his debts, he uses three books, the memorandum for general information on the day-to-day business transactions, from which daily such information is entered briefly in the journal using debit and credit. In Venice they used the term "Per" [meaning "from"] indicating the debtor (*debitore*) and "A" [meaning "to"] denoting the creditor (*creditore*). A journal entry might then be "Per Cash//A Capital", "Cash" being debited by the first journal entry (the two lines serving as a separation), and "Capital" being credited by the second journal entry. This information could then be transferred to the ledger, the debit being placed on the left under a Cash heading and the credit to the right under a Capital heading. At a given time such as

---

[3] Lauwers, L. and M. Willekens "Five Hundred Year of Bookkeeping. A Portrait of Luca Pacioli," *Tijdschrift voor Economie en Management*, Vol. XXXIX, 3, 1994, 289-304.)

Statue of Fra Luca Pacioli at his birthplace in Sansepolcro.

the year-end, the total of the amounts of the debits must equal the total of the amounts of the credits, giving the bookkeeper in effect a trial balance.

"The first generally accepted evidence for the application of double-entry bookkeeping derives from the communal account books of the City of Genoa in the year 1340." During the 1380s this method grew in popularity among merchants.[4]

At no place did Pacioli claim originality for the double-entry system of book-keeping which he described. He specifically stated that he was merely writing down the system which had been used in Venice for over two hundred years.

"Pacioli's Venetian Accounting" is still the foundation of "the universal standard for accounting in the Western world" — today.[5]

John B. Geijsbeek's (1914) publication on "Ancient Double–Entry Bookkeeping," relying on E.L. Jäger's (1876) German translation of Pacioli's *Particularis de computis et scripturis*, contains an interesting introduction by Page Lawrence (1914), a C.P.A. in Denver, Colorado, lamenting the lack of accounting principles and a dissonance between

---

[4] Arlinghaus, Franz-Josef. "Double-Entry Bookkeeping" in Medieval Italy: En Encyclopedia." Online at http://www.franzarlinghaus.de/ Bookkeeping.html. Retrieved 2010-07-10.
[5] Weis, 1991.

the accounting academic and accounting practitioner in the education and training of the "embryo accountant" at American — not British [and Canadian] — universities. Lawrence's introduction is a refreshing read, and is reprinted for the benefit of accounting and finance educators unedited in its entirety in the Appendix.

Accounting is at the cross-roads, being an art based on a *known* man-made convention; hardly a science in the abstract based on research. The Financial Accounting Standards Board (FASB), as well as the International Accounting Standards Board (IASB) and other Institutes, have excelled in producing a historical-backward-looking *complexity* of rules and regulations where underlying dynamic-forward-looking *simplicity* is required.

Internationally active monetary financial institutions have been "certified" to comply with this *complexity* at year end, only to collapse months later, magnifying the Global Financial Crisis of 2008; and we are still in the midst of it.

The educational issue of academically *versus* professionally qualified accounting educators is addressed by American and Canadian colleges and universities by giving preference to instructors with both qualifications. Many, if not most, accounting professors are MBA/PhDs *and* CPAs or CAs.

Michael Schemmann
Nakhon Ratchasima
July 2010

PARTICULARIS DE COMPUTIS ET SCRIPTURIS [6]

DETAILS OF CALCULATION AND RECORDING [7]

CHAPTER 1.

THINGS THAT ARE NECESSARY TO THE GOOD MERCHANT AND THE METHOD OF KEEPING A LEDGER WITH ITS JOURNAL, IN VENICE AND ELSEWHERE.

In order that the subjects of His Illustrious Highness, the most honorable and magnanimous Duke of Urbino (D. U. D. S.—*Docis Urbini Domini Serenissimi*)[8], may have all the rules that a good merchant needs, I decided to compile, in addition to the subjects already treated in this work, a special treatise which is much needed. I have compiled it for this purpose only, *i.e.*, that they (the subjects) may whenever necessary find in it everything with regard to accounts and their keeping. And thereby I wish to give them

---

[6] The eleventh *tractatus* of the ninth *distinctio* of Pacioli's *Summa de Arithmetica, Geometria, Proportioni et Proportionalità* entitled *Particularis de computis et scripturis*. (Lauwers, L. and M. Willikens. "Five Hundred Years of Bookkeeping. Tijtschrift voor Economie en Management, Vol. XXXIX, 3, 1994, 289-304, online at https://lirias.kuleuven.be/bitstream/ 123456789/119065/1/TEM1994-3_289-304p.pdf. Retrieved 2010-07-10.

[7] Wikipedia "Accountancy" online at http://en.wikipedia.org/wiki/ Accountancy, retrieved 2010-07-10. Geijsbeek translated as "Particulars of Reckonings and Recordings."

[8] NOTE—Throughout the text, the words in parentheses are the English translator's, as also the punctuation and paragraphing, as the original is extremely deficient in these. The words in italics are copied exact from Pacioli's original.

enough rules to enable them to keep all their accounts and books in an orderly way. For, as we know, there are three things needed by any one who wishes to carry on business carefully. The most important of these is cash or any equivalent, according to that saying, *Unum aliquid necessarium est substantia.* Without this, business can hardly be carried on.

It has happened that many without capital of their own but whose credit was good, carried on big transactions and by means of their credit, which they faithfully kept, became very wealthy. We became acquainted with many of these throughout Italy. In the great republics nothing was considered superior to the word of the good merchant, and oaths were taken on the word of a good merchant. On this confidence rested the faith they had in the trustworthiness of an upright merchant. And this is not strange, because, according to the Christian religion, we are saved by faith, and without it it is impossible to please God.

The second thing necessary in business is to be a good bookkeeper and ready mathematician. To become such we have given above (in the foregoing sections of the book) the rules and canons necessary to each transaction, so that any diligent reader can understand it all by himself. If one has not understood this first part well, it will be useless for him to read the following.

The third and last thing is to arrange all the transactions in such a systematic way that one may understand each one of them at a glance, i. e., by the debit (*debito*—owed to) and credit (credito—owed by) method. This is very essential to merchants, because, without making the entries systematically it would be impossible to conduct their business, for they would have no rest and their minds would always be troubled. For this purpose I have written this treatise, in which, step by step, the method is given of making all sorts of entries. Although one cannot write out every essential detail for all cases, nevertheless a careful mind will be able, from what is given, to make the application to any particular case.

This treatise will adopt the system used in Venice, which is certainly to be recommended above all the others, for by means of this, one can find his way in any other. We shall divide this treatise in two principal parts. The one we shall call the Inventory, and the other Disposition (arrangement). We shall talk first of the one and then of the other, according to the order contained in the accompanying Table of Contents, from which the reader may take what he needs in his special ease.

He who wants to know how to keep a ledger and its journal in due order must pay strict attention to what I shall say. To understand the procedure well, we will take the ease of one who is just starting in business, and tell how he must proceed in keeping his accounts and books so that at a glance he may find each thing in its place. For, if he does not put each thing in its own place, he will find himself in great trouble and confusion as to all his affairs, according to the familiar saying, *Ubi non est ordo. ibi est confusion* (Where there is no order, there is confusion). In order to give a perfect model to every merchant, we will divide the whole system, as we have .said, in two principal parts, and we will arrange these so clearly that one can get good results from them. First, we will describe what the inventory is and how to make it.

CHAPTER 2.

FIRST PART OF THIS TREATISE, WHICH IS CALLED INVENTORY—WHAT INVENTORY IS, AND HOW TO MAKE IT.

First, we must assume that every action is determined by the end in view, and in order to pursue this end properly, we must use every effort. The purpose of every merchant is to make a lawful and reasonable profit so as to keep up his business. Therefore, the merchants should begin their business with the name of God at the beginning of every book and have His holy name in their minds. To begin with, the merchant must make his inventory (*inventario*) in this way: He must always put down on a sheet of paper or in a separate book whatever he has in this world, personal property or real estate, beginning with the things that are most valuable and most likely to be lost, such as cash, jewels, silver, etc., for the real estate, such as houses, lands, lakes, meadows, ponds, etc., cannot be lost as personal property. Then all the other things must be put down one after another. In the said inventory give always first the day, the year, the place and your name. This whole inventory must be completed in one day, otherwise there will be trouble in the future in the management of the business.

As an example for you, I will give you, now, an idea as to how the inventory is to be made, so that you may' use it as a guide in any particular ease.

CHAPTER 3.

EXAMPLE OF AN INVENTORY WITH ALL ITS FORMAL REQUIREMENTS.

In the name of God, November 8th, 1493, Venice.

The following is the inventory of myself, N. N., of Venice, Street of the Holy Apostles.

I have written down systematically, or had written by Mr. So-and-So, this inventory of all my property, personal and real, what is owed to me (*debiti*), and what is owed by me (*crediti*), of which I on this said day find myself possessed in this world.

First Item: First I find myself possessed in cash, in gold and coin of so many ducats, of which so many are Venetian, and so many gold Hungarian; of so many large florins made up of Papal, Siennese and Florentine, etc. The rest consists of many different kinds of silver and copper coins, *i.e.*, *troni*, *marcelli*, papal and royal *carlini* and Florentine *grossi*, and Milanese *testoni*, etc.

Second Item: I also possess, in set and unset jewels, so-and-so many pieces, among which are many *balassi* set in gold, rings weighing so-and-so-many ounces, carats, grains, etc., per piece or in bulk, etc., which you can express in any manner you wish. There are so-and-so-many sapphires set on clamps for women; they weigh so much. And there are so-and-so-many rubies, unset, weighing so much. The rest consists of unpolished pointed diamonds, etc. Here you may give such descriptions and weight as you desire.

Third Item: I have clothes of many kinds; so many of such kind; and so many of such-and-such kind, etc., describing their condition, colors, linings, styles, etc.

Fourth Item: I have several kinds of silverware, as cups, basins, *rammi, cosileri, piromi,* etc. Here describe all the different kinds one by one, etc., and weigh each kind diligently. Keep an account of pieces and weights, and of the alloy, whether the Venetian or the one used at Ragusa, etc. Also mention the stamp or mark that they might have.

Fifth Item : I have so much *massaria dei lini*—that is, bed sheets, table cloths, shirts, handkerchiefs, etc., so many of each. Of the bed sheets, so many are made three-piece sheets, and so many are three and one-half, etc., mentioning whether the linen is Padua linen or some other kind, new or used; length so many *braccia,* etc.; so many shirts, etc.; table cloths of so many threads; so many big handkerchiefs and so many small, mentioning whether new or used, giving the different kind in your own way.

Sixth Item: I have so many feather beds and their respective pillows, mentioning whether the feathers are new or used, whether the pillow-cases are new or used, etc., which altogether or one by one weigh so much, marked with my mark or with some other mark, as the custom is.

Seventh Item: I have at home or in the store so much goods of different kinds: First, so many cases of ginger *michino,* weighing so many pounds, marked with such-and-such mark, and so on, describing each kind of said goods with all their marks that you might possibly give and with all the possible accuracy as to weight, number, measurement, etc.

Eighth Item: I have so many cases of ginger *bellidi,* etc., and so many sacks of pepper, long pepper or round pepper, depending on what it is ; so many packages of cinnamon, etc., that weigh so much ; so many packages of cloves, etc., that weigh so much, with *fusti polvere* and *cappellitti* or without, etc., and so many pieces of *verzini* weighing so much, and so much sandalwood, red or white, weighing so much, and so on, entering one item after another.

Ninth Item: I have so many skins for coverings, that is, so many white kids and so many *albertoni* or *marchiani*, etc., so many of such-and-such kind, etc., so many fox skins, so many tanned and so many raw, so many chamois skins tanned, and so many raw.

Tenth Item: I have so many fine skins, *fore armenti*, *dossi varii*, *zebelini*, etc., so many of such-and-such

kind, and so many of such-and-such kind—defining diligently and truthfully each time' so that truth will always guide you, etc., distinguishing the things that ought to be entered by pieces from those that ought to be entered by weight, and those that ought to be entered by measurement, because in these three ways business is conducted everywhere ; certain things are reckoned by the bushel, others by the hundreds, others by the pound, others by the ounce, others by number, others by a *conto* (by single numbers) as leather goods or skins, others by the piece, as precious stones and fine pearls, etc. ; so you will make a notation of each thing. These examples will serve as a guide for all the rest, etc.

Eleventh Item: I have in real estate: first, a house with so many stories, so many rooms, court yard, wells, garden, etc., situated in St. Apostle Street over the Canal, etc., adjoining such-and-such parties, etc., giving the names of the boundary line properties, making reference to the oldest and most reliable deeds, if there are any; and so, if you have more houses in different localities, you will enter them in a similar way.

Twelfth Item: I have so many pieces of land under cultivation (fields or *staiore* or *panora*) etc., entering them by the name according to the usage of the country where you are, saying where they are situated, etc., as, for instance, a field of so many *tavole*, or *canne*, or *pertiche*, or *bevolche*, etc., situated in such-and-such town in the Province of Padua or somewhere else, adjoining the land of so-and-so, giving all the boundary lines and referring to deeds or the description from the recorder's office, for which land you pay taxes in such-and-such municipality, which are worked by so-and-so with a yearly income of so much, and so on; you will enter all your possessions, etc., cattle, etc.

Thirteenth Item: I have in deposit with the Camera de I'Impresti (a bank), or with another bank in Venice, so many ducats; or with the parish of Canareggio, etc., or part in one parish and part in another, giving the names under which they have been deposited, mentioning the book of the bank, the number of the page where your account is, and the name of the clerk who keeps said book, so that you can easily find your account when you go to get money, because in such offices they must keep very many accounts on account of the big crowd that sometimes goes there, and you must also .see that dates are put down precisely so that you know when everything falls due and what the per cent. is.

Fourteenth Item: I have so many debtors (*debitori*): one is so-and-so, who owes me (*me dee dare*—shall give me) so many ducats, and so on, giving the names of each one, putting down all annotations as to the names, their family names, and how much they owe you (*te debbono dore*—shall have to give you) and why; also whether there are any written papers or notarial instruments. In total I have so many ducats to collect, you will say, of good money, if the money is due from good people, otherwise you will say of bad money.

Fifteenth Item: I am debtor in total to the extent of so many ducats, etc. I owe so many to so-and-so. Here mention your creditors (*creditori*) one by one, writing down whether there are any documents or writings or instruments; if possible, mention the persons present when the debt was incurred, the reason, the time and the place, for any case that might arise in court or out of court.

CHAPTER 4.

VERY USEFUL ADMONITION AND GOOD ADVICE TO THE GOOD MERCHANT.

And so, as we have said, you shall enter diligently every thing that you have, whether personal property or real estate, one by one, even if there were ten thousand items, putting down the condition and nature, whether deposited or loaned, etc. You will have to mention each thing in proper order in the said Inventory with all marks, names, surnames—as far as possible—for things are never too clear to a merchant on account of the different things that may happen in business, as anybody in business knows. Right is the proverb which says: More bridges are necessary to make a good merchant than a lawyer can make. Who is the person that can count all the things that can happen to a merchant—on the sea, on land, in times of peace and abundance and times of war and famine, in times of health or pestilence ? In these crises he must know what to do, in the marketplaces and in the fairs which are held now in one place and now in another. For this reason it is right to say that the merchant is like a rooster, which of all the animals (*animale*) is the most alert and in winter and summer keeps his night vigils and never rests. And they say of the nightingale that it sings throughout the whole night; however, this may be in the summer during the hot weather, but not during the winter, as experience shows. Also it is said that the head of the merchant has a hundred eyes, and still they are not sufficient for all he has to say or to do. These things are told by people who have had experience in them, such as the Venetians, Florentines, Genoans, Neapolitans, Milanese, people of Ancona, Brescia, Bragama, Aquila, Sienna, Lucca, Perugia, Urbino, Forosempronio, Cagli, Ugubio, Castello, Brógo, Fuligno, Pisa, Bologna, Ferrara, Mantua, Verona, Vincenza, Padua, Trani, Lecce, Bitonto, which are among the first cities of Italy and have the first place in commerce—especially the cities of Venice and Florence, which adopt rules that respond to any need. And well say the municipal laws: *Vigilantibus et non dormientibus jura subveniunt*—which means, The law helps those that are awake, not those that sleep. So in the divine functions of the Holy Church they sing that God promised the crown to the watchful ones, and this was the instruction that Virgil gave to Dante as to his son, in Canto 24 of the Inferno, where he exhorts him to the work by which one can reach the hill of virtue: Now, my son, it behooves that you quit your laziness, said my master, for he who lies on feathers or under covers will never amount to anything. Whoever spends his life in this way, he said, will leave on this earth the same trace as the smoke in the air or foam on the water, etc.; and another Italian poet admonishes us in the same way, saying: Work should not seem to you strange, for Mars never granted a victory to those that spent their time resting. And it is also very good to quote that sage who said to the lazy man to take the ant as an example; and the Apostle Paul says that no one will be worthy of the crown except he who shall fight valiantly for it.

24

I wanted to bring in these reminders for your own good, so that the daily care about your business would not seem heavy to you, especially the writing down everything and putting down every day everything that happens to you, as we shall unfold in the next chapters. But above all, remember God and your neighbor; never forget to attend to religious meditation every morning, for through this you will never lose your way, and by being charitable, you will not lose your riches, as the poet says: *Nec caritas, nec Missa minuit iter*, etc. And to this our Savior exhorts us in the book of St. Matthew, when he says: *Primum quaerite regulum dei, et haec omnia adiicietur vobis*, which means: Seek you, Christians, first the kingdom of God and then the other temporal and spiritual things you will easily obtain, because your Heavenly Father knows very well your needs, etc.

And this I hope will be sufficient as an instruction for you to make the Inventory, etc., and to do other things well.

CHAPTER 5.

SECOND PRINCIPAL PART OF THIS TREATISE NAMED DISPOSITION (ARRANGEMENT)—WHAT IS UNDERSTOOD BY IT—WHAT IT CONSISTS OF IN BUSINESS, AND THE THREE PRINCIPAL BOOKS OP THE MERCHANT.

Comes now the second principal part of this treatise, which is called disposition, and of this I have to talk more at length than of the first part, in order to make it very clear. I will divide it in two parts. We shall call the one, *Corpo overo monte de sutto el trafico*; the other, *Corpo overo monte de botega* (Commerce in general, and Your store in particular).

. First, we shall speak of commerce in general and its requirements. Immediately after the Inventory, you need three books to make the work proper and easy. One is called Memorandum (*Memoriale*), the second Journal (*Giornale*), and the third Ledger (*Quaderno*). Many, on account of their small business, use only the last two, that is, the journal and the ledger.

We shall speak about the first—that is, of the memorandum book, and thereafter of the other two, about their makeup, and how they should be kept. First of all, we will give the definition of the memorandum book.

CHAPTER 6.

OF THE FIRST BOOK, WHICH IS CALLED MEMORANDUM BOOK (MEMORIALE), OR SCRAP BOOK [*SQUARTA LOGLIO*), OR BLOTTER (*VACHETTA*). WHAT IS UNDERSTOOD BY IT AND HOW ENTRIES SHOULD BE MADE IN IT AND BY WHOM.

The memorandum book, or, according to others, scrap book or blotter, is a book in which the merchant shall put down all his transactions, small or big, as they take place, day by day, hour by hour. In this book he will put down in detail everything that he sells or buys, and every other transaction without leaving out a jot; who, what, when, where, mentioning everything to make it fully as clear as I have already said in talking about the Inventory, so that there is no necessity of saying it over again in detail. Many are accustomed to enter their inventory in this book, but it is not wise to let people see and know what you possess. It is not wise to enter all your personal property and real property in this book. This book is kept on account of volume of business, and in it entries should be made in the absence of the owner by his servants, or his women if there are any, for a big merchant never keeps his assistants idle; they are now here, now there, and at times both he and they are out, some at the market place and some attending a fair, leaving perhaps at home only the servants or the women who, perhaps, can barely write. These latter, in order not to send customers away, must sell, collect or buy, according to the orders left by the boss or owner, and they, as well as they can, must enter every transaction in this memorandum book, naming simply the money and weights which they know; they should note the various kinds of money that they may collect or take in or that they may give in exchange. As far as this book is concerned, it is not as important to transfer to standards the various kinds of coin handled as it is with the journal and ledger, as we will see hereafter.

The bookkeeper will put everything in order before he transcribes a transaction in the journal. In this way, when the owner comes back he will see all the transactions, and he may put them in a better order if he thinks necessary. Therefore, this book is very necessary to those who have a big business. It would be too much trouble to put down in a beautiful and orderly way every transaction immediately after it take place, in books which are authentic and kept neat with care. You must make a mark on the cover of this book, as well as on all the others, so that you can distinguish them when, in the process of the business, the book is filled or has served for a certain period of time and you take another book. You must take another book when the first one has been used entirely, yet many are accustomed in different localities to balance annually these books although they are not full; and they do likewise with the other books not yet mentioned, as you will see hereafter.

On the second book you should put another mark different from the first, so that at any' time you can trace your transaction easily. For this purpose we use the date. Among true Christians there is the good custom to mark their first books with that glorious sign from which every enemy of the spiritual flees and before which all the infernal spirits justly tremble—that is, the holy cross, by which in our tender years we begin to learn to read. The books that follow, you may mark in alphabetical order, calling A the second, and B the third, etc. So that we call the first books with the Cross, or Memorandum with Cross, and the second Memorandum A, Journal A, Ledger A. The pages of each of these books ought to be marked for several reasons known to the merchant, although many say that this is not necessary for the Journal and Memorandum books. The transactions are entered day by day, one under the other, in such way that it may be easy to trace them. This would be all right if all the transactions of one day would not take more than one page; but, as we have seen, for many of the bigger merchants, not one, but several pages have to be used in one day. If some one would wish to do something crooked, he could tear out one of the pages and this fraud could not be discovered, as far as the dates are concerned, for the days would follow properly one after the other, and yet the fraud may have been committed. Therefore, for this and other reasons, it is always good to number and mark each single page in all the books of the merchants; the books kept in the house or kept in the store.

CHAPTER 7.

OF THE MANNER IN WHICH IN MANY PLACES MERCANTILE BOOKS ARE AUTHENTICATED, WHY AND BY WHOM.

All these books, according to the good customs of several countries where I have been, should be taken and shown to a certain mercantile officer such as the Consuls in the City of Perosa employ, and to him you should state that those are the books in which you intend to write down, or somebody else write down for you, all your transactions in an orderly way; and also state in what kind of money the transactions therein should be entered—that is, whether in *lire di Picioli*, or in *lire di Grossi*, or in *ducats* and *lire*, etc., or in *florins* and *denari*, or in ounces, *tari*, *grani*, *denari*, etc. The good merchant should put down these things always on the first page of his book, and if afterwards the handwriting should be done by somebody else than the one stated at the beginning of the book, this should be recorded at the office of the said officer. The clerk should mention all this in the records of the said officer—that is, on such and such a day you presented such and such books, marked with such and such mark, which books are named, one so-and-so, the other so-and-so, etc.; of which books one has so many pages, another so many, etc., which books you said would be kept by you or by so-and-so; but that it may be that in said Memorandum Book or Scrap Book or Blotter, some person of your family might enter said transaction, as explained before. In this ease, the said clerk shall write down on the first page of your books, in his own handwriting, the name of the said officer, and will attest to the truth of everything and shall attach the seal of that office to make the books authentic for any case in court when they might be produced.

This custom ought to be commended exceedingly ; also the places where the custom is followed. Many keep their books in duplicate. They show one to the buyer and one to the seller, and this is very bad, because in this way they commit perjury. By presenting books to the said officer, one cannot easily lie or defraud. These books, after they have been carefully marked and authenticated, shall be kept in the name of God in your own place, and you are then ready to start your business. But first you shall enter in an orderly way in your Journal all the different items of the Inventory in the way that I will tell you later. But first you must understand how entries should be made in this Memorandum Book.

CHAPTER 8.

HOW ENTRIES SHOULD BE MADE IN THE SAID MEMORANDUM BOOK, AND EXAMPLES OF THE SAME.

We have said already, if you will remember, that any one in your family can make entries in the said Memorandum Book, or Scrap Book or Blotter. Therefore, it cannot be fully stated how the entries should be made, because some members of your family will understand and some will not. But the common custom is this: Let us say, for instance, that you bought several pieces of cloth—for instance, 20 white *bresciani*, at 12 ducats apiece. It will be enough simply to make the entry in this way: On this day we have or I have bought from Mr. Filippo d'Rufoni of Brescia, 20 pieces of white *bresciani*. These goods are at Mr. Stefauo Tagliapietra 's place; one piece is so long, according to the agreement, and paid for at so many ducats, etc., marked with such and such number, etc. You mention whether the cloth is *a trelici*, or *a la piana*, wide or narrow, fine or medium, whether the Bergamo kind, or Vincenza, or Verona, or Padua, or Florence, or Mantua. Also you have to state here whether the transaction was made through a broker and whether it was made in cash entirely or part only in cash and part on time, stating the time, or whether it was part in cash and part in trade. In this ease you must specify the things that were given in exchange, number, weight, measurement, and the price of the bushel or of the piece, or of the pound, etc., or whether the transaction was all by payment on time, stating the time when the payment should be made, whether on *Galia de Barutta*, or on *Galia de Fiandra*, or on the return day of a ship, or on the date of some fair, or other festivity, as for instance, on the next harvest day or on next Easter, or on next Christmas, or on Resurrection day or Carnival day, etc., according to what was understood in the transaction. Finally, I must say that in this memorandum book nothing should be omitted. If it were possible, it should be noted what many others had said during the transaction because, as we have said about the Inventory, the merchant never can be too plain.

CHAPTER 9.

OF NINE WAYS IN WHICH THE MERCHANT USUALLY BUYS, AND THE GOODS WHICH IT IS MORE OR LESS NECESSARY TO BUY ON TIME.

Since we are talking about buying, you must know that usually you can make your purchase in nine ways—that is: either in cash or on time; or by exchanging something, which is usually called a trade; or partly in cash and partly on time—or partly in cash and partly by trading and partly on time; or by draft (*assegnatione de ditta*); or partly by draft and partly on time, or partly by draft and partly by trading. In these nine ways it is customary to make purchases. If you would make your purchases in some other way you must state in your memorandum book with precision the way that you have made the purchase, or have somebody else do it for you, and you will do well.

You buy on time usually when you buy *guati* or oats, wines, salt, remnants from a butcher shop, and fats. In these cases, the seller promises to the buyer to give all the guati that he will have in that season. The butcher will sell you and promises to give you all the hearts, skins, fat, etc., that he will have during that year. This kind for so much a pound, that kind for so much a pound, etc., and similarly for the fat of beef, of mutton, etc.; the black skins of mutton at so much apiece; and the white mutton skins, etc., and so with the oats, or *guati*; you must specify the price for each bushel or other measure and the kind of oats as is the custom at Chiusi de Perugia. In buying *guati* you must see whether they are of our city San Sepolcro, or Mercatello, or Sant' Angelo, or Citta de Costello, or Forli, etc.

In this memorandum book, whether kept by you or by others, you must mention every single point. You state the things in a simple way as they happened, and then the skillful bookkeeper, after four or five days, or eight days, may enter all these transactions from the said memorandum book into the Journal, day by day; with this difference, though, that it is not necessary for him to put down in the Journal all the long lines of words that were used in the memorandum book, because it is sufficient to put them down in an abridged way, and besides, references should always be made from one book to the other. Those that are used to keeping these three books in the way we have said never must enter one thing in Journal if they have not first entered it in the memorandum book. This will be enough as to the arrangement of the said memorandum book, whether it is kept by you or others. Remember that there are as many ways to buy as to sell; therefore, I need not explain the ways of selling, because you knowing of the ways of buying can understand the selling.

CHAPTER 10.

THE SECOND IMPORTANT MERCANTILE BOOK WHICH IS CALLED JOURNAL; WHAT IT IS, AND HOW IT SHOULD BE KEPT IN AN ORDERLY WAY.

The second common mercantile book is called the Journal (*Giornale*) which, as we have said, must have the same mark that is on the memorandum book and the pages marked as we have said in talking of the memorandum book.

Always at the beginning of each page you must put down the date, and then, one after another, enter all the different items of your inventory.

In this Journal, which is your private book, you may fully state all that you own in personal or real property, always making reference to the inventory papers which you or others may have written and which are kept in some box, or chest, or *filza*, or *mazzo*, or pouch, as is customary and as is usually done with letters and other instruments of writing.

The different items entered in the said Journal ought to be entered there in a neater and more systematic way, not too many or too few words, as I will show in the few following examples. But first of all you must know that there are two words or expressions (*termini*) necessary in the keeping of a Journal, used according to the custom of the great City of Venice, and of these I will now speak.

CHAPTER 11.

THE TWO EXPRESSIONS USED IN THE JOURNAL, ESPECIALLY IN VENICE. THE ONE CALLED "PER," AND THE OTHER "A," AND WHAT IS UNDERSTOOD BY THEM.

As we have said, there are two expressions (*termini*) used in the said Journal; the one is called "per," and the other is called "a," each of which has a meaning of its own. "Per" indicates the debtor (*debitore*) one or more as the case may be, and "a," creditor (*creditore*), one or more as the case may be. Never is any item entered in the Journal which also is to be entered in the Ledger, without preceding it by one of the two expressions. At the beginning of each entry, we always provide "per," because, first, the debtor must be given, and immediately after the creditor, the one separated from the other by two little slanting parallels (*virgolette*), thus, //, as the example below will show.

CHAPTER 12.

HOW THE ENTRY SHOULD BE MADE INTO THE JOURNAL BY MEANS OF THE DEBIT AND THE CREDIT, WITH MANY EXAMPLES. THE TWO OTHER EXPRESSIONS USED IN THE LEDGER, THE ONE CALLED "CASH," AND THE OTHER "CAPITAL." AND WHAT SHOULD BE UNDERSTOOD BY THEM.

With the name of God you shall begin to enter into your Journal the first item of your Inventory, that is, the quantity of cash that you possess, and in order to know how to enter this Inventory into the Ledger and Journal, you must make use of the two other expressions (*termini*); the one called "cash" (*cassa*) and the other "capital" (*cavedale*). By cash is understood your property or pocketbook (*borscia*: from *bursa*, or bag); by capital is understood the entire amount of what you now possess.

This capital must always be placed as creditor (*creditore*) in all the principal mercantile Ledgers and Journals and the cash always debtor. Never at any time in the management of your business may cash be creditor, but only debtor unless it balances. For if, in balancing your book, you find that cash is in the credit, it would denote a mistake in the book, as I will remind you hereafter at its proper place. Now this entry ought to be made in the Journal, and ought to be arranged in this way:

EXAMPLE OF MAKING AN ENTRY IN THE JOURNAL.

FIRST. November 8, MCCCCLXXXXIII in Venice.

Debit 1.	Per cash // A—Capital of myself so and so, etc. In cash I have at present, in gold and coin, silver
Credit 2.	and copper of different coinage as it appears in the first Inventory in cash, etc., in total so many gold ducats and so many silver ducats. All this is 1 our Venetian money; that is counting 24 *grossi* per ducat and 32 *picioli* per *grosso* in gold is worth: L... (*Lire*), S... (*Soldi*), G... (*Grossi*), ...(*Picioli*).

For the second item you shall say this way:

SECOND. Per mounted and unmounted precious stones of several kinds //. A capital ditto for so many mounted *belassi*, etc., weighing, etc., and so many sapphires, etc., and rubies and diamonds, etc., as the said Inventory shows to which, according to current prices I give these values: *Belassi* worth, etc.; and so you shall state a price for each kind in total that are worth so many ducats. Their value is

L..., S..., G..., P....

After you have once named the day, the debtor and the creditor, you may say for brevity—if you don't make any other entry in between: On the day ditto, per ditto, // a ditto.

THIRD. Per silver //. A ditto—by which capital is understood—for several kinds of silver which at present I possess—that is, wash basins so many, so many coppers, so many cups, so many *pironi*, and so many *cosilier*, etc., weighing in total so much. Their value is:

L..., S..., G..., P...

You shall give all the details in entering these items for everything as you have them in the Inventory, giving to each thing a customary price. Make the prices rather higher than lower; for instance, if it seems to you that they are worth 20, you put down 24, so that you can make a larger profit; and so you will enter everything, putting down for each thing its weight, number, value, etc.

L..., S..., G..., P...

FOURTH. Per woolen clothes //. A ditto, for so many clothes of such and such color, etc., of such and such style, etc., lined, etc., new or used, etc., for myself or for my wife or for my children, I give the total value, according to the current price, so many ducats. And for cloaks, so many of such and such color, etc., and so on, for all the other clothes:

L..., S..., G..., P...

FIFTH. Per linen //. A ditto, for so many bed sheets, etc., and put down their number and value as the Inventory shows:

L..., S..., G..., P...

SIXTH. Per feather beds //. A ditto, etc., for so many feathers—and here put down all that the Inventory shows, number and value: L..., S..., G..., P...

SEVENTH. Per ginger //. A ditto, for so many packages, etc., giving all the details that are contained in the Inventory, number, value, according to common prices, etc., so many ducats: L..., S..., G..., P...

In this way you can continue to enter all the other items, making a .separate entry for each different lot, and as we have .said before, giving the current prices, number, marks, weights, as the Inventory shows. Indicate only one kind of money, to which you reduce the estimated values. In the column for the amounts, only one kind of money should appear, as it would not be proper to have appear in this column different kinds of money.

You shall close each entry in the Journal by drawing a line from the end of the last word of your descriptive narrative (explanation) up to the column of the figures. You shall do the same in the memorandum book, and as you transfer an entry into the Journal from the memorandum book, yon shall draw a single diagonal line (*una sola riga a traverso*) through it in this way /; this will show that this item has been entered (*posta*) in the Journal.

If you should not draw this line through the entry, you shall cheek off (*lanciarai*) the first letter of the beginning of the entry, or the last letter, as we have done at the beginning of this; or otherwise you shall use some other sign by which you will understand that the said item has been transferred into the Journal. Although you may use various and divers expressions or marks, nevertheless you must try to use the common ones which are used by the other merchants, so that it will not look as if you would deviate from the usual mercantile custom.

CHAPTER 13.

THIRD AND LAST PRINCIPAL MERCANTILE BOOK CALLED THE LEDGER. HOW IT IS TO BE KEPT. ITS ALPHABET (INDEX), AND HOW THIS CAN BE KEPT SINGLE AND DOUBLE.

After you have made all your entries in the Journal in an orderly way, you must transfer them to the third book, called Ledger (*Quaderno Grande, i.e.*, big book). This Ledger contains usually twice as many pages as the Journal. In it there must be an alphabet or repertory or "*trovorello*" (finding key) according to some; the Florentines call it "*Stratto*." In this index you shall write down all the debtors and creditors in the order of their initial letter, together with the number of their respective pages. You shall put the names that begin with A in the A page, etc.

This Ledger, as we have said before, must bear the same sign or mark that is on the Journal and memorandum book: its pages should be numbered ; and at the top at the right margin as well as at the left margin, you shall put down the date. On the first page you shall enter each as debtor. As in the Journal, so in the Ledger, cash should be entered on the first page. It is customary to reserve the whole of the first page to cash, and not to enter anything else either under the debit (in *dare*) or the credit (in *havere*). This because the cash entries are more numerous than all others on account of almost continuously paying out and receiving money ; therefore, it needs much space. This Ledger must be ruled, and should have as many lines as there are kinds of money that you want to enter. If you enter *lire, soldi, denari* and *picioli*, you shall draw four lines, and in front of *lire* you shall draw another line in order to put in the number of the pages of the Ledger debit and credit entries.

Before these lines you shall draw two more lines wherein to mark the dates as you go on, as you have seen in the other books, so that you may find each item quickly. This book shall also bear the sign of the cross as the others.

CHAPTER 14.

HOW THE ENTRIES SHOULD BE TRANSFERRED FROM THE JOURNAL INTO THE LEDGER AND WHY, FOR EACH ENTRY OF THE JOURNAL, YOU HAVE TO MAKE TWO IN THE LEDGER; HOW ENTRIES IN THE JOURNAL SHOULD BE CANCELLED. THE TWO NUMBERS OF THE PAGES OF THE LEDGER WHICH ARE PLACED IN THE MARGIN OF EACH ENTRY AND WHY.

For each one of all the entries that you have made in the Journal you will have to make two in the Ledger. That is, one in the debit (*in dare*) and one in the credit (*in havere*). In the Journal the debtor is indicated by per, the creditor by a, as we have said. In the Ledger you must have an entry for each of them. The debitor entry must be at the left, the creditor one at the right; and in the debitor entry you must indicate the number of the page of the respective creditor. In this way all the entries of the Ledger are chained together and you must never make a credit entry without making the same entry with its respective amount in the debit. Upon this depends the obtaining of a trial balance (*bilancio*) of the Ledger.

There can not be a closing [balance—Editor] (*saldo*) because there must be as much in credit as there is in debit. In other words, you shall add together all the debit entries, even if there are ten thousand, on a separate sheet, and then

add together in the same way all the credit entries; the totals
of the one should be the same as the totals of the other;
otherwise it would show that some mistake has been made
in the Ledger. We will speak at length about this when we
talk about the way of making the trial balance (*bilancio*).
And since for one entry of the Journal you make two in the
Ledger, you shall draw two diagonal lines as you make the
transfer—that is, if you first transfer the debit entry, you
shall first draw a diagonal line (*riga a traverso*) at the
beginning of the entry in the Journal which shows that the
entry has been posted (*posta*) to the debit into the Ledger. If
you transfer the credit entry, either at this time or later, as it
often happens that the bookkeeper can make two or three
entries on the same page in order to prevent his coming
back to write on that same page—in which case he should
draw a line at the right side where the entry terminates. This
will show that the entry has been transferred to the credit of
the Ledger. These two lines, you may see in the preceding
diagram, drawn in the margin by the first cash entry; the
one is called debit line, and the other credit line. At the side,
in the marginal part, you shall write down two numbers
before the beginning of the entry, the one under the other.
The upper indicates at what page of the Ledger the debit
entry is, and the lower indicates the page of the Ledger
where the credit is, as you will see at the cash entry in the
above example, like this ½, [but—Editor] without a line
between them. Some are accustomed to draw a line in
between, like this, ½. This does not matter, but it looks
nicer without the line between, so that the figures will not
appear to the reader as if they were fractions. The upper
figure, 1, means cash was entered in the first page of the
Ledger, and capital was entered in the second page of the
said Ledger; the cash on the debit, and the capital on the
credit side. You should know that the closer to the debtor

you can place the creditor, the nicer it will look. It is just the same, however, no matter where it is; but it may look bad on account of the date which at times must be put between entries, and it makes it difficult then to find the dates. We can not tell you everything fully, but you with your natural ingenuity must guide yourself. Therefore you always try to put the said creditor immediately after its debtor on the same line or on the line immediately following without entering anything else in between, for whenever there is a debit item there must exist at the same time a credit item. For this reason, get the one as near as possible to the other.

CHAPTER 15.

THE WAY IN WHICH THE CASH AND CAPITAL ENTRIES SHOULD BE POSTED IN THE LEDGER IN THE DEBIT AND THE CREDIT. THE DATE WHICH AT THE TOP OF THE PAGE IS WRITTEN DOWN ACCORDING TO THE ANCIENT USE. CHANGING OF THE SAME. HOW TO DIVIDE THE SPACE ON THE PAGES FOR SMALL AND LARGE ACCOUNTS AS THE BUSINESS REQUIRES.

After having told you these things for your instruction, we write now the first entry of the cash in the debit column, and then the first entry of the capital in the credit column, in the Ledger. But, as we have said, you shall write down in the Ledger the year in the old way by using the alphabet, thus: MCCCCLXXXXIII, etc. It is not customary to put the day at the top in the Ledger as in the Journal, because one account in the Ledger may have several dates, and therefore you can not keep the dates in order by putting them at the top ; but you shall put the days in the body of the entry, as you will understand hereafter.

We put the day to one side, in the space of which I have spoken, just before the entry. If an item refers to a transaction which happened in a different year than that written at the top of the page, which happens when one does not balance and transfer his books at the end of each year, then this year shall be put on the side, in the margin near the entry of the item to which it refers. This only happens in the Ledger, and can not happen in the other books. In making this entry for the year, use the antique letters, which are neater, although it does not matter very much.

Thus, you shall put it this way:

JESUS MCCCCLXXXXIII.

Cash is debtor (*dee dare*—shall give) on November 8, "per" capital. On this day I have in moneys of different kinds, gold and other coins; page 2: L.X^m, S... , G... , P...

Here you do not need to be very lengthy if yon have already given the description in the Journal. Try to be very brief.

At the beginning of the page we say more, but in the entries following it is enough to say: on ditto, "per" such and such; page, etc.,   L... , S... , G... , P...

After you have made the entry in this way, you shall cancel in the Journal as I have explained to you. Then in the credit side you shall write down this way:

JESUS MCCCCLXXXXIII.

Capital of myself, so and so, is creditor (*dee havere*—shall have) on November 8, "per" cash. On this day I have in cash, in gold and other kinds of money; page 1:

This entry is also sufficient; express yourself briefly for the reason above said. If there are other items to be entered in the same account, it will be enough to say, on ditto, "per" such and such, etc., as has just been shown. At the end of this treatise, I will give you an example, and thus you will go on expressing yourself briefly especially in those things which are private—that is, of which you do not have to give an account to any one. But as to other things for which you have to give an account to other people, it will be better for you to be more explicit, although for explanations we always rely on the Journal. Then you will cancel, by drawing a line, the credit entry in the Journal as I have said above in Chapter 12. In the margin, just opposite the entry, you shall write down the two numbers of the pages where the debit and credit entries are. That is, you should put the number of the debit page above, and the number of the credit page below, as we have done above in the cash entry. Then you shall at once enter in the alphabet or repertory (index) this debtor and this creditor, each one under its own letter as I have told you before. That is, cash at the letter C, by saying in this way: Cash, page 1. And capital also at the letter C, saying: Capital belonging to me, page 2. And so on, you shall enter (in this repertory) all the creditors under their respective letters, so that you may find them easily in the Ledger mentioned.

Take notice, that if by any chance you should lose this Ledger through robbery, or fire, or shipwreck, etc., if you have either of the other two books, that is, the memorandum book or Journal, you can, by means of this book always make up another Ledger with the same entries, day by day, and enter them on the same pages on which they were in the last book ; especially so, if you have the Journal in which, when .you transferred the different entries into the Ledger, you wrote down at the margin the two numbers of the debit entry page, and the credit entry page, the one above the other, which two numbers indicated the pages of the ledger where the two entries had been entered. In this way you can duplicate your Ledger. This is enough said for the posting of one entry.

For the second entries, which pertain to precious stones, you shall enter in the Ledger as follows:

FIRST, without my telling it to you over again, you shall write down at the top of the page the date, if there has been no date written before because of another account, for at times on the same page two or three accounts are made. Sometimes you won't give much space to one special account because you know that you will not have to use that account over again. Therefore you will give to this account a smaller space than the space you give to other accounts which you had to use more, as we have said above in Chapter 13, when talking about cash and capital, to which we give the whole page, as we have to use these two accounts very often because of the many transactions. This is done in order to lessen transfers.

Now then, after you have found the proper place (in the ledger), you shall write down on the left—because the debtor must always be at the left: Precious stones of many kinds debit (*dienno dare*—shall give), on November 8, per capital, for so many pieces, etc., weighing so much, so many are counted *balassi*, etc., and so many sapphires, etc., and so many rubies, etc., and so many unpolished diamonds in bulk (or divide the different kinds), for a value of so many ducats; page 2:   L40; SO; GO; PO.

You shall cancel this item in the Journal on the debit side by drawing a line as I have told you in Chapter 12. And then you will go to capital, and you shall enter this entry with fewer words, for the reasons above expressed in this chapter, writing it down on the credit side under the first entry that you have already made, and you shall express yourself this way:

On the day, or ditto, for precious stones of several kinds, as it appears at page 3 :   L40 ; SO ; GO ; PO.

After which you shall draw another line on the credit side of the Journal, as I have shown in Chapter 12 ; you shall put down in the margin the two numbers of the pages of the Ledger in which you have made these entries, one above the other, as I have told you. We shall say, for instance, that you have entered the debit entry at page 3 ; the capital entry will still appear at page 2, as long as that page is not filled.

This example will guide you in other cases. After you have made the entries in the Ledger and marked it in the Journal, you shall put it at once in the index as I have told you above in this chapter—that is, under the letter G or Z, according as to how *Gioie* (stone) is pronounced. In Venice the custom is to pronounce it with Z; in Tuscany, with G. Guide yourself according to your own understanding.

CHAPTER 16.

HOW THE ENTRIES RELATIVE TO THE MERCHANDISE OF WHICH ONE IS POSSESSED ACCORDING TO HIS INVENTORY, OR OTHERWISE, SHOULD BE MADE IN THE LEDGER BOTH IN THE DEBIT AND THE CREDIT.

You will be able to transfer easily by yourself from the Inventory to the Journal the four items of your personal goods—that is, silver, linen, feather beds, clothes, etc., exactly as you write them in the Inventory, as we explained in Chapter 6. This Inventory was not contained in the memorandum book, for the reasons therein expressed. And as to how to make these entries in the Journal and the Ledger, and as to how to record them in the Index, I will leave to your ability, on which I count very much. We shall proceed to enter in the Journal, as well as in the Ledger, the seventh item (of the Inventory), which pertains to Ginger. This must be a sufficient instruction for you by which to make any other entry relative to your merchandise. You should always have in mind their number, weights, measurements and values according to the different ways in which it is customary to make purchases or sales among merchants in the Rialto, or elsewhere. It is not possible to give here full examples for all these operations, but from those few that we give here you will be able to understand how to go ahead in any other case. For if we wanted to give you an example of all the ways in which merchants do business in Trani, Lecce, Bari and Bitonto—-that is, to give you the names of their weights, measurements, etc., and also to tell you about the ways that they use them in Marca and in our Tuscany, this would make our treatise very long, which, on the contrary, I intend to make short. As to this seventh item to be entered in the Journal, we shall proceed thus : Per Ginger in bulk or package—you shall express yourself as you like— // a ditto—by which capital is understood, because you have already mentioned it in the entry immediately preceding, when you entered your second item from the inventory, that is, precious stones—as we said in Chapter 12—I possess on this day so many packages weighing so much, or 1 possess so many pounds, if in bulk, according to the current prices, of a value by the hundred or by the pound, of so many ducats ; in total I give them the value of so many ducats.   L... , S... , G... , P...

After you have entered it in the Journal in this way, you shall cancel it in the memorandum book or inventory, as we have said in Chapter 12, and you shall do the same for the other items. Of this entry, as we have said, as well as of any entry made in the Journal, you shall make two different entries in the Ledger; that is, one in the debit and the other in the credit.—See Chapter 14. In making the entry in the Ledger in the debit, you shall proceed in this way : First you shall put the year, in ease there is none, at the top of the page, without there putting down the day, for, as we have said in Chapter 15, it is not customary to put down the day at the beginning of the page of the Ledger because on that same page several entries may be made under the debit and credit which, while belonging to the same year, refer to transactions made in different months and days. Even if on that page of the Ledger there was only one cash entry or other entry, the day put at the top of the page could not be very well kept because, under the said entry, it would be necessary to write down transactions which happened in different months and days. For this reason the ancient people never put the day at the top of the pages in mercantile ledgers, as they saw that there was no justification for it, etc. You shall make this entry in the debit (in the Ledger) in the following manner: Ginger in bulk, or so many packages, debit {dee dare—shall give) on November 8 per capital, for so many pieces, weighing so many pounds, which I on this day have in my store, or at home in my house, and which according to current prices are worth so many ducats and in total so many ducats, grossi, picioli, etc.; Page 2:   L... , S... , G... , P...

Then you shall cancel this entry on the debit side of the Journal—that is, at the left, as I have told you often, and then you shall enter it on the credit side under Capital, as I have shown you in entering the precious stones item in Chapter 15, that is:

On ditto per Ginger in bulk or packages, etc.; Page 3:
                              L... , S... , G... , P...

After you have entered it in this way, you shall cancel the entry on the credit side of the Journal—that is, at the right—as I have shown you before, and you shall also write down at the margin the numbers of the respective pages of the Ledger one above the other—that is, three above and two below, as you have made the debit entry at Page 3 and the credit entry at Page 2, and you shall thereafter enter it in the alphabet or repertory under its respective letter, which may be Z or G, for the reasons given in the preceding chapter.

CHAPTER 17.

HOW TO KEEP ACCOUNTS WITH PUBLIC OFFICES, AND WHY. THE CAMERA DE L'IMPRESTI (MUNICIPAL LOAN BANK) IN VENICE, WHICH IS MANAGED BY *SESTIERI* (DISTRICTS).

I shall not give you any more rules for the other items—that is, leather goods for coverings, tanned or raw, etc., for each of which you shall make entries in the Journal and Ledger, carefully writing down everything and checking off, etc., without forgetting anything, because the merchant must have a much better understanding of things than a butcher.

If you have accounts with the Camera de L'Impresti, or with other banks, as in Florence, or with the Monte de La Dote, in Genoa, as well as similar offices or bureaux with which you have business, see that you keep these accounts very clearly and obtain good written evidence as to debits and credits in the handwriting of the clerks in those institutions. This advice you will carefully follow, for reasons to be explained in chapter on documents and letters. Because in these offices they often change their clerks, and as each one of these clerks likes to keep the books in his own way, he is always blaming the previous clerks, saying that they did not keep the books in good order, and they are always trying to make you believe that their way is better than all the others, so that at times they mix up the accounts in the books of these offices in such way that they do not correspond with anything. Woe to you if you have anything to do with these people. Therefore, be very careful when dealing with them, and be observant at home and keep your head in the store. Maybe they mean well, nevertheless they may show ignorance. In this way you shall keep accounts with the *Gabellari* and *Datiarii* (revenue officers) as to the things that you might sell or buy, things that you grow, things that you plant, etc., as it is the custom in Venice where people are used to keeping an account through the office of the *Messetaria* (market master or exchange), some at 2%, some at 1%, some at 4%. You should mention the book of the broker through whom the transaction was made, and also mention the special mark that the broker has in this book—that is, the book in which he makes a record of the market transaction at said office which they call "*Chiamans*" in Venice. For each broker has a book in the said office, or a place in some book in the said office, in which he has to make a record of all the transactions which he has with the citizens of the town or with outsiders. If the broker should not do that he would be fined and dismissed.

And justly the glorious republic of Venice punishes them and their clerks who should misbehave. I know of many who in the past years have been heavily punished, and right they are in having one officer whose only duty is to oversee all these officers and their books whether they are well kept or not, etc.

CHAPTER 18.

HOW YOU SHOULD KEEP YOUR ACCOUNTS WITH THE OFFICE OF THE MESSETARIA IN VENICE. HOW TO MAKE ENTRIES PERTAINING THERETO IN THE MEMORANDUM BOOK, JOURNAL AND LEDGER, AND ABOUT LOANS.

When you want to do business with the said offices, you shall always charge to the Camera de L'Impresti (municipal loan bank) so many per cent, on all your funds or capital, naming the district where one resides. Likewise, for the amount of the daily sales for many are the sales made for you or for others, as those people know who are familiar with the Rialto. Be careful to put down the name of the party that buys and his place of business, etc. When you withdraw said funds, you shall always credit the said bank, day by day and district by district.

In doing business with the office of the *Messetaria* (exchange), you shall keep the account in this way: When you buy any merchandise through brokers, you shall credit the said office of the *Messetaria* with the 2% or 3% or 4% of the whole amount, and shall charge it to that specific merchandise, for you are thus paying for it, etc. Therefore the buyer, when he makes his payments to the seller, should always retain that percentage, no matter whether the payments are made in cash or otherwise, as the said office does not concern itself about anything except the rate (%) to which it is entitled. The brokers make a report of the transaction, how and what for and with whom made, in order to have things clear in case any question should arise, which may happen.

A common proverb says : Who does nothing, makes no mistakes; who makes no mistakes learns nothing, etc.

If any question should arise and the parties wish to settle it, they would go and examine the records of the transaction made by the broker, to which records, according to the public decrees, as full faith is given as to a public notarial document, and according to these records very often the office of the Consuls of the merchants issues its judgment.

I say, then, when you buy anything, you must always know what is due to the *Messetaria*, and you withhold half of this from what you pay to the seller; that is, if the particular thing that you buy is subject to a 4% payment to that office, as per public decrees of the Republic, you withhold 2% of what you give to the seller. You give him that much less in order that he receives what is due him. You then will become a debtor for the whole amount which is due the said office, and you shall credit the said office with it in your Ledger when you keep an account with that office and charge it to the goods that you have bought, as we have said, because that office does not interest itself in the party who sells out, but in the party who buys. In accordance with this, the buyer will be allowed to take out of the official warehouses merchandise in proportion to the brokerage paid and according to their books kept at the shipping counter, whether it came by land or sea. Therefore, the merchants should keep a careful account with the said office so that they know how much merchandise they can take out. They are not allowed to take out more than they have bought unless they have paid the extra brokerage.

Of these purchases, I will give you here an example and how the transaction with the said office must be recorded in the Journal and in the Ledger. First, you shall express yourself in the memorandum book in the following manner:

I (or we), on this day above mentioned, have bought of Mr. Zuan Antonio, of Messina, so many boxes of Paler- mo sugar and so many loaves of the net weight—that is, without the boxes, wrappers, ropes and straw—so many pounds at so many ducats per hundred; I deduct for what is due to the *Messetaria* at the rate of so much per cent., so many *ducats, grossi. picioli* etc. The broker was Mr. Zuan de Gaiardi; net value, so many *ducats, grossi. picioli.* paid in cash.

The same should be entered in the Journal in the following manner:

Per Palermo sugar // A cash. Cash paid to Mr. Zuan Antonio of Messina for so many boxes and so many loaves, of the net weight—that is, without the boxes, wrappers, ropes and straw—so many pounds; at so many ducats per hundred, it amounts to so many ducats; I deduct what is due to the *Messetaria* at so much per cent., so many ducats, etc. ; net residue, so many ducats, etc. The broker was Mr. Zuan de Gaiardi.   L... , S... , G... , P...

In the Ledger you shall make the entries as follows: Palermo sugar debit (*dee dare* or shall give) cash. Cash paid to Mr. Zuan Antonio of Messina for so many boxes and so many loaves, weighing, net, so many pounds, at so many ducats per hundred, which amounts to—Page 1:

L... , S... , G..., P...

And you shall credit cash with the same amount, and shall always credit the *Messetaria* with twice the amount which you withhold from the price paid to the seller—that is, for the commission due by the seller and by you.

Immediately after, you shall make another entry crediting the said office with the said sugar and charging the said merchandise. This will do for a purchase by cash. Now we shall consider one made partly in cash and partly on time.

First, in the memorandum book you shall say as follows: By cash and on time on such and such day, I have bought on the said date of Mr. Zuan Antonio of Messina so many loaves of Palermo sugar, weighing net so many pounds, at so many ducats per hundred, making a total of so many ducats. This is in part payment; for the rest I shall have time to pay until the whole month of August next, etc. The broker was Mr. Zuan Gaiardi.

You must understand that you do not need to have a written paper containing the terms of the transaction, for the broker shall record that in the said Office. This record is enough for you, but as a precaution, sometimes people require a contract.

You will make the entry in the Journal as follows: First you shall credit Mr. So-and-So for the total amount, and then charge him for the money that he has received.

JESUS 1493

On such and such a day of such and such month, etc., per Palermo sugar / so many loaves, weighing net so many pounds at so many ducats per hundred, making a total of so many ducats ; deducting for his share of the brokerage at so much per cent., so many ducats, leaving a net balance of so many ducats, of which now I have to pay so many, and as to the rest I have time until the end of next August. The broker was Mr. Zuan de Gaiardi; value: L... , S... , G... , P...

Immediately after, credit the office of the Messetaria with the commission due to it : Per ditto // A Office of the *Messetaria*. For the amount above mentioned—that is, so many ducats at the rate of so much per cent, for my share and for the share of the debtor (seller), in all amounting to so many *ducats, grossi, picioli*: value: L... , S... , G... , P...

For the cash payment, you shall charge him and credit cash in the following manner:

Per Mr. Zuan Antonio of Messina // A cash. By cash paid him for part payment of said sugar according to the terms of the transaction, so many ducats, as it appears from his receipt written in his own handwriting. Value:

L... , S... , G... , P...

In the Ledger you shall write down as follows:

Palermo sugar debit (*dee dare*—shall give) on such and such a day of November, per Zuan Antonio of Messina, for so many loaves, weighing net so many pounds, etc., at so many ducats per hundred, making a total, net of the brokerage ; Page 4: L... , S... , G... , P...

These items shall be entered in the credit column as follows:

Mr. Zuan Antonio of Messina, credit (*dee havere*—shall have), per Palermo sugar so many loaves, weighing net so many pounds, at so many ducats per hundred, amounting, net of the brokerage, so many ducats, of which I must now pay so many ducats, and for the rest I have time until the end of next August. Broker, Mr. Zuan de Gaiardi ; Page 4 ; value: L... , S... , G... , P...

For the cash payment you shall put in the debit column:

Mr. Zuan, debit {dee dare—shall give), on such and such a day, etc., per cash to him paid for part payment on sugar—I received from him according to our agreement—so many ducats, as it is shown by his own handwriting in his book; page 1: L... , S... , G... , P...

The account of the Messetaria in the Ledger shall be as follows:

Office of the Messetaria, credit (*dee havere*—shall have), on such and such day, per Palermo sugar bought from Mr. Zuan Antonio, of Messina, for the amount of so many ducats, at so many ducats per hundred. Broker, Mr. Zuan de Gaiardi ; Page, etc.: L... , S... , G... , P.../

A Mr. Zuan Antonio, of Messina, for

CHAPTER 19.

HOW WE SHOULD MAKE THE ENTRIES IN OUR PRINCIPAL BOOKS OF THE PAYMENTS THAT WE HAVE TO MAKE EITHER BY DRAFT OR THROUGH THE BANK.

And as to the purchases, this should be sufficient to guide you, whether the payment of the purchase should be made all in cash or part in cash and part on time; or part in cash or part by bill of exchange or draft (*ditta*); or all through the bank; or part in cash and part through the bank; or part through the bank and part on time; or part through the bank and part by bill of exchange; or part through the bank, part in cash, part by bill of exchange and part by merchandise, etc.

For in all these ways it is customary to make purchases, and in each case you shall make entries, first in the Day Book, then in the Journal, then in the Ledger, taking as a guide the foregoing example.

But when you make a payment part through the bank and part by bill of exchange, deliver first the bill of exchange and then settle through the bank, which is safer. Many observe this precaution on good grounds, whenever they have to make payments part in cash to settle this balance through the bank, etc. If you make payments part through the bank, part by trading something or part by a bill of exchange and. part in cash, you shall charge the seller for all these things and you shall credit each of the said things, each thing in its own place.

Now that you know how to go ahead whenever you make purchases, you will also know what you have to do when you sell. In this ease, you shall charge the different buyers and shall credit the different goods that you sell and shall charge cash if you get money for the same, and you shall charge bills of exchange if you get a bill of exchange in payment, and credit the latter when the bank pays the exchange.

Therefore, referring again to the purchase, you shall credit the purchaser with all that he gives you in payment, etc.

This will be enough for your instruction on this subject.

CHAPTER 20.

ENTRIES FOR THE WELL-KNOWN AND PECULIAR MERCANTILE CUSTOMS OF TRADING AND PARTNERSHIP, ETC. HOW THEY SHOULD BE ENTERED IN THE MERCANTILE BOOKS. FIRST: SIMPLE TRADINGS, THEN COMPLEX TRADINGS AND EXAMPLES OF ENTRIES FOR THEM IN THE MEMORANDUM BOOK, JOURNAL AND LEDGER.

Now we shall speak of how certain well-known and peculiar entries should be made which are of the highest importance in commerce, and which usually are kept separate from the others so that they can show their respective profits and losses (*pro e danno*). They cover tradings, partnerships, suggested business trips, trips on your own ventures, commissions from others, drafts (*ditta*) or bills of exchange (*bancha descritta*), actual trades, store accounts, etc. I will tell you briefly about these accounts, how you should make the entries in your books so that you don't get mixed up in your affairs.

First, we shall show how to enter a trade (*barato*). Trades are usually of three kinds, as we said in Section 9 of

Treatise III,[9] Pages 161 to 167, where it is stated fully and you can refer to it.

I say, therefore, that no matter how you make a record of the trade in your books, you shall first enter it in the memorandum book, stating in detail all about it, its terms and conditions and whether it was made through a broker. After you have so described it, you then at the end shall put a money value on it; and you shall put down such price in accordance with the current value which the things that you have traded have; reckoning in any kind of money in the memorandum book. Afterwards the bookkeeper, when he transfers the entry to the Journal and Ledger, will reduce that money to the standard money that you have adopted.

This is done because, without entering the value of the things that you have traded, you could not, from your books and accounts, learn, except with great difficulty, what your profit or loss is. The merchandise must always be reduced to actual money value in order to take care of it (in the books).

You may keep a separate account of the goods received in trade, if you wish to do that, in order to know how much you make out of them separate from those of the same kind that you might already have at home, or separate from those that you might get after that, in order to know which was the best transaction. You also may keep only one account of all the goods—for instance, if you have already some ginger, and you get some more ginger through a trade. In this case you shall make the entries in the Journal as follows:

Per Ginger in bulk or in packages // A sugar, such and such kind, so many packages, weighing so many pounds. Received from a trade for sugar in this manner: I valued the

---

[9] This book is Treatise XI of Section 9 of the *Summa de arithmetica, geometria, proportioni et proportionalita* [Editor].

sugar 24 ducats per hundred, of which I should receive one-third in cash, and I valued the ginger at so many ducats per hundred. The said sugar is in so many loaves weighing so many pounds, worth 20 ducats per hundred, and for the said ginger I received so many pounds of sugar and so many loaves, and their value is: L... , S... , G... , P...

And if you do not know exactly how many loaves of sugar you have received for the said ginger, it does not matter, because you may correct the mistake in the following entry, whether the mistake was made plus or minus, or correct it through the cash entry. On the contrary, you know exactly the weight and money value, and you lose nothing in either by not knowing the number of loaves. It is not always possible to keep an account of all small details.

Now you will debit cash for whatever cash you received, and you shall credit sugar in the following manner:

Per Cash // A ditto. In the said trade I received cash from so and so for so many loaves of sugar weighing so many pounds; value: L... , S... , G... , P...

You shall record in the Journal direct all these different items soon after the trade is made, and should take the name of the merchandise if you do not want to keep a separate account; but if you want to keep them in a separate account, you will write this way in the Journal:

Per ginger *bellidi* received by trade from so and so, etc. // A sugar, etc., stating everything as shown above. In the Ledger then they will have separate accounts.

This will be sufficient for you for all kinds of trades.

Luca Pacioli

CHAPTER 21.

THE OTHER WELL-KNOWN ENTRY CALLED PARTNER-
SHIP. HOW IT SHOULD BE WRITTEN IN EACH BOOK IN THE
PROPER MANNER.

The other well-known entry is the buying of anything
in partnership (*compra* or *compagnie*—may also mean joint
venture but not corporation) with other people, such as
silks, spices, cotton, dyes, or money exchanges, etc. These
accounts must all be entered in all three books separately
from your own. In the first, that is, the memorandum book,
after writing down the date at the top, you shall state in a
simple way all the purchases with terms and conditions,
referring to papers or other instruments that you might have
made, stating for how long it was made and what were its
objects, mentioning the employees and apprentices that you
should keep, etc., and the share, and how much each of you
puts in the business, whether in goods or cash, etc., who are
the debtors and who are the creditors. You should credit the
partners (*compratori*) for the amount which each of them
contributes, and you shall debit cash with the same if you
keep the account with your own. But it is better for the
business if you keep this cash account separate from your
private one when you are the one at the head of the
business, in which ease you should have a separate set of
books in the same order and way we have shown
previously. This will facilitate things for you. However, you
might keep all these accounts in your own personal books
opening new accounts which, as we have said, are referred
to as well-known accounts because they are kept separate
from all the others, and I will show here how to enter them
in your Day Book and then in the Journal and Ledger—but
if you keep separate books, I will not give you any further

instruction, because what I have said so far will be sufficient for you—you shall do as follows: On this day we have made a contract with so and so, and so and so, jointly, to buy (*facto compra*) wool, etc., under terms and conditions, etc., as appears from such and such paper or such and such instrument, for so many years, etc. So and so put in as his share, so much in cash; the other put so many bales of French wool, weighing net so many pounds, etc., estimated at so many ducats per, etc. The third, so and so, put in so many credits, namely, one for so many ducats, etc.

Then, in the Journal, putting everything in its own place, you shall imagine that you have a partnership's cash (*cassa de compagnia*) and a partnership's capital (*cavedale de compangnia*) ; so that in each entry you make, you shall always name the accounts of the partnership so that you can distinguish them from your own entries. First, you make the cash entry, and then follow it systematically by the other entries:

Per Partnership cash // A such and such partner's account—so that if you have other accounts, you will not get confused—so and so put in on this day as his share according to our agreement as appears from the contract, etc.; value: L... , S... , G... , P...

Then you shall mention the other things that they have contributed:

Per French wool // A partner's account, for so many bales weighing in total, net, so many pounds, as examined by all of us, at so many ducats per bushel, according to the terms of the contract we have made, etc., worth in total so many ducats ; value: L... , S... , G... , P...

And so on for the other different items, and as to the due bills which have been put in the Company, you shall state this way:

Per Mr. So and So, Partnership's account // A so and so, according to our agreement, which so and so transferred to the Partnership as a good due bill of so many ducats:

L... , S... , G... , P...

Now that I have given you a kind of introduction to these new entries, I won't go any further, as it would be a very tiresome thing to repeat all I have said.

And I will not say anything as to the way in which to make these entries in the Ledger, as I know it will be easy for you to know what should be entered as debit and what as credit from the Journal. You shall enter them accordingly as I have told you at Chapter 15, and shall cancel these entries in the Journal as T told you at Chapter 12, always writing in the margin just opposite them the number of the debit and credit pages of the Ledger, and as you enter them in the Ledger you shall also enter them in the index, as I have told you repeatedly before.

CHAPTER 22.

REGARDING THE ENTRIES OF EVERY KIND OF EXPENSE, AS FOR INSTANCE HOUSEHOLD EXPENSES, ORDINARY OR EXTRAORDINARY, MERCANTILE EXPENSES, WAGES OF CLERKS AND APPRENTICES. HOW THEY SHOULD BE ENTERED IN THE BOOKS.

Besides the entries so far mentioned, you shall open these accounts in your books : that is, mercantile expenses, ordinary household expenses, extraordinary expenses, and account for what is cashed in (*entrata*) and what is paid out (*uscita*) ; one for profits and loss (*pro e danno*—favor and damages) or (*avanzi e desavanzi*—increase and deficit), or (*utile e danno*—-profit and damage) or (*guadagno e perdita*—gain and loss), which accounts are very necessary at any time so that the merchant can always know what is his capital and at the end when he figures up the closing (*sado*), how his business is going.

I will show here clearly enough how these accounts should be kept in the books. The account named "small business expenses" is kept because we can not enter every little thing in the account of the merchandise that you sell or buy. For instance, it may happen that after a few days, for these goods that you sell or buy, you will have to pay the porter, the weigher, the packer, the shipper and the driver, and others, paying to this one 1 penny, to the other one 2 pennies, etc. ; if you want to keep a separate account for each of these different transactions, it would be too long and too expensive. As the proverb says:

De minimis non curat Praetor (Officials do not bother with details). And it may be that you will have to employ those same people—drivers, porters, shippers and packers—for different things, as, for Instance, you may need them for loading the several merchandises in a seaport, and you will employ them and will have to pay them for all these services at one time, and you could not charge the several kinds of merchandise with its proportion of these expenses. Therefore you open this account which is called "small business expenses," which is always used in the debit as are all the other expenses. You enter in this account the salaries of your store employees, although some keep a separate account of the salaries that they pay so that they know how much they pay for salaries every year, etc. This should also always appear as a debit. If the account should be in credit, this would show that there is a mistake. Therefore you shall say as follows in the memorandum book:

On this day we have paid to drivers, shippers, packers, weighers, etc., who loaded and unloaded such and such goods, so many ducats, etc.; then in the Journal you shall say as follows:

Per small business expenses // A cash. Cash paid for boats, ropes, etc., for such and such goods in total, so many ducats; value: L... , S... , G... , P...

In the Ledger, you shall state as follows:

Small business expenses (*dee dare*—shall give) debit per cash on this day, etc., value; page, etc.

L... , S... , G... , P...

We can not do without the account of ordinary household expenses. By these expenses we mean expenses for grains, wine, wood, oil, salt, meat, shoes, hats, stockings, cloths, tips, expenses for tailors, barbers, bakers, cleaners, etc., kitchen utensils, vases, glasses, casks, etc.

Many keep different accounts for all these different things, so that they can see at a glance how each account stands, and you may do so and open all these different accounts, and any accounts that you like, but I am talking to you about what the merchant can not do without. And you shall keep this account in the way I have told you to keep the small business expense account, and make each entry day by day as you have such expenses, as for grain, wine, wool, etc. Many open special accounts for these different things so that at the end of the year or at any time they may know how much they are paying out; but for the small accounts, as meat, fish, boat fares, etc., you shall set aside in a little bag one or two ducats and make small payments out of this amount. It will be impossible to keep an account of all these small things.

In the Journal you shall state so:

Per household expenses // A cash. Cash set aside in a little bag for small expenses, so many ducats, value:

L... , S... , G... , P...

If you wish, you can include in the household expenses the extraordinary expenses, as those that you make for amusements or that you lose in some game, or for things or money that you might lose, or that might be stolen or lost in a wreck or through fire, etc., for all are classified as extraordinary expenses. If you want to keep a separate account for them, you may do so, as many do, in order to know at the end of the year how much you have expended for extraordinary expenses, under which title you should include also gifts and presents that you might make to any one for any reason. Of these expenses, I will not speak any longer, because I am sure that you, keeping in mind what we have said so far, will know how to manage yourself. And leaving this subject, I will tell you of the way to open your store accounts in the Ledger and in the other books as if you wanted to conduct a store for your own account. I shall tell you that you must pay good attention, for it is a very nice thing for you to know.

CHAPTER 23.

IN WHAT MANNER THE ACCOUNTS OF A STORE SHOULD BE KEPT. WHETHER THE STORE IS UNDER YOUR CARE OR UNDER THE CARE OF OTHER PEOPLE. HOW THE ACCOUNTS SHOULD BE ENTERED IN THE AUTHENTIC BOOKS OF THE OWNER SEPARATE FROM THOSE OF THE STORE ITSELF.

I say then that if you should have a store outside of your house (branch store) and not in the same building with your house, but which you have fully equipped, then for the sake of order you should keep the accounts in this way: You should charge it in your books with all the different things that you put into it, day by day, and should credit all the different merchandise that you put in it also each one by itself, and you must imagine that this store is just like a person who should be your debtor for all the things that you may give (*dai*) it or spend for it for any reason. And so on the contrary you shall credit it with all that you take out of it and receive from it (*cavi e recevi*) as if it were a debtor who would pay you gradually. Thus at any time that you so desire, you may see how the store is running—that is, at a profit or at a loss—so you will know what you will have to do and how you will have to manage it. There are many who in their books charge everything to the manager of the store. This, however, can not be done properly without the consent of that person, because you can never enter in your books as a debtor any person without his knowing it, nor put him as a creditor under certain conditions without his consent. If yon should do these things, it would not be right and your books would be considered wrong.

As to all the fixtures which you might put in said store necessary to the running of it according to the circumstances—if you had for instance a drug-store, you would have to furnish it with vases, boiling pots, copper utensils, with which to work—you shall charge your store with all this furniture. So all of these things you shall charge, and he who is at the head of the store shall make a proper inventory of all these things in his own handwriting or in the handwriting of somebody else, at his pleasure, so that everything should be clear. And this will be sufficient for a store whose management you may have turned over to somebody or to some of your employees. But if you want to run the store yourself, you shall do as I will tell you and it will be all right. Let us suppose that you buy and do all of your business through the said store and do not have to take care of any other business, then you shall keep the books as I have said before, whether you buy or sell. You shall credit all those that sell goods to you on time, if you buy on time, or credit cash if you buy for cash, and charge the store; and if you should sell at retail, as when the sale should not amount to four or six ducats, and so on, then you shall keep all these moneys in a small drawer or box from which you shall take it after eight or ten days, and then you shall charge this amount to cash and shall credit the store; and you shall make this entry as follows:

Per various merchandise sold—for which you shall have kept an account—and so on. I shall not talk at length about this because I have given you sufficient explanation previously and you know how to go ahead by this time. For accounts are nothing else than the expression in writing of the arrangement of his affairs, which the merchant keeps in his mind, and if he follow this system always he will know all about his business and will know exactly whether his business goes well or not. Therefore the proverb: If you are in business and do not know all about it, your money will go like flies—That is, you will lose it. And according to the circumstances you can remedy what is to be remedied; for instance, if necessary, you might open other accounts. And this will be sufficient for you.

CHAPTER 24.

HOW YOU SHOULD KEEP IN THE JOURNAL AND LEDGER. THE ACCOUNTS WITH THE BANK. WHAT IS UNDERSTOOD BY THEM. BILLS OF EXCHANGE—WHETHER YOU DEAL WITH A BANK OR YOURSELF ARE A BANKER. RECEIPTS FOR DRAFTS—WHAT IS UNDERSTOOD BY THEM AND WHY THEY ARE MADE OUT IN DUPLICATE.

In respect to banks, which you can find nowadays in Venice, in Bruges, in Antwerp, Barcelona, and other places well known to the commercial world, you must keep your accounts with them with the greatest diligence.

You can generally establish connections with a bank. For instance, you may leave your money with the bank as a place of greater safety, or you may keep your money in the bank as a deposit in order to make therefrom your daily payments to Peter, John and Martin, for a bank draft is like a public notarial instrument, because they are controlled by the state.

If you put money in the bank, then you shall charge the bank or the owner or partners of the bank and shall credit your cash and make the entries in the Journal as follows:

For Bank of Lipamani // A cash. Cash deposited with so and so by me, or others, for my account, on this day counting gold and other money, etc., in all so many ducats; value: L... , S... , G... , P...

And you will have the banker give you some kind of a written record for your surety; if you make other deposits you shall do the same. In ease you should withdraw money, the banker shall have you write a receipt; in this way, things will be kept always clear.

It is true that at times this kind of receipt is not given, because, as we said, the books of the bank are always public and authentic ; but it is better to require this writing, because, as I have told you, things can't be too clear for the merchant.

If you want to keep this account in the name of the owners or partners of the bank, you may do so, as it is the same thing, because, if you open the account under the name of the bank, by the bank you mean the owners or the partners. If you keep it under the name of the owners, you shall say this way:

Per Mr. Girolimo Lipamani, banker, and associates—if there are many— // A cash—and here you write as above.

In your books you shall always mention all agreements, terms, conditions that there might be; also instruments of writing and places where you keep them, whether file box, pouch or trunk, so that you may easily find them, as these papers should be diligently kept for an everlasting memorial of the transaction (*ad perpetuam memoriarn*) on account of dangers.

As you may have several different business relations with the bankers for yourself, or for others, you must keep various accounts with them so that you won't mix one thing with another, and avoid confusion, and in your entries you shall say: On account of such and such thing, or on account of so and so, or on account of goods, or on account of cash deposited in your name or in the name of others, as we have said. You will know yourself how to make these entries. In the same way you will proceed in case others should turn money over to you for some account ; you shall charge that account in your book—that is, you shall charge the bank, stating whether it was in part payment or in full, etc., and you shall credit the person that gave you the money. This will be all right.

When you should withdraw money from a bank either to pay somebody else as part payment or payment in full, or to make a remittance to parties in other countries, you shall do in this case just the opposite of what we just said—that is, if you withdraw money you shall charge your cash and credit the bank or owners of the bank for the amount withdrawn; and if you should give an order on the bank for somebody else, you shall charge this party and credit the bank or owners of the bank for that much, stating the reasons. You shall enter the cash item in your Journal as follows:

Per cash // A bank, or Mr. Girolimo Lipamani, for cash which on this day or on such and such day I withdrew for my need, in all so many ducats, value:

L... , S... , G... , P...

And if you should issue an order in favor of Mr. Martino, for instance, you shall say thus:

Per Martino on such and such a day // A ditto for ditto for cash, etc., for so many ducats, for which I gave an order, in part payment or in full payment, or for a loan, etc., on this day; value: L... , S... , G... , P...

Every time you transfer these entries from the Journal Into the Ledger, you shall also record them in the Index and cancel them, as I have shown you, adding more or less words according to the facts in the case.

You must do the same in case you want to send drafts elsewhere, as to London, Bruges, Rome, Lyons, etc. You shall mention in the letter the terms, conditions, etc., whether these drafts are at sight or at a certain date or at pleasure of the payor, as it is customary, mentioning also whether it is a first, second, third draft, etc., so that no misunderstanding can occur between you and your correspondent, mentioning also the kind of money in which you draw or transmit, their value, the commission, the costs and interest that might follow a protest—in a word, everything must be mentioned, why and how.

I have told you how you have to proceed in dealing with a bank. If on the contrary you are the banker you have to do in the opposite way (*mutatis mutandis*); when you pay you charge the man to whom you pay and credit cash. If one of your creditors, without withdrawing money, should Issue a draft to somebody else, you shall say in the Journal as follows: Per that special creditor of yours // A the man to whom the money was assigned. In this way you just make the transfer from one creditor to another and you still remain as debtor and act as a go-between, as witness or agent of the two parties. For ink, paper, rent, trouble and time you get a commission, which is always lawful, even though through a draft there is no risk of travel, or the risk when money should be transferred to third parties, etc., as in actual exchanges, of which we have spoken in its place. If you are a banker, whenever you close an account with your creditors always remember to get back all the papers, documents or other writings in your own handwriting that they might have. When you issue any such paper always mention it in your books so that when the time comes you will remember to ask for them and to destroy them so that nobody else should appear with these papers and ask money for the second time. You must always require good receipts as those do who are accustomed to this kind of business. For the custom is this: If you, for instance, come from Geneva to Venice with a draft on Messrs. Giovanni Frescobaldi & Co., of Florence, which draft might be at sight or on a certain date or at your pleasure, and the amount were for a hundred ducats, that is, for as many ducats as you have paid to the drawer of the draft, then the said Messrs. Giovanni & Co., when they honor the draft and give you the cash will require you to give two receipts written in your own handwriting, and if you should not know how to write, a third party or a notary public will make them out. He will not be satisfied with one because he has to send one to the banker at Geneva, who wrote him to pay the hundred ducats to you for his account just to show that he honored his request, and for this purpose he will send to the other banker a letter enclosing your receipt written in your handwriting. The other receipt he will keep for himself on file so that in balancing with the other banker, the banker could not deny the transaction, and if you should go to Geneva you could not complain of him or of Mr. Giovanni for if you should complain he would show you your receipt written by yourself and you would not play a beautiful part in it. All these precautions ought to be taken by necessity on account of the bad faith of the present times. Out of these transactions two entries ought to be made in the Ledger, one entry in the account with Mr. Giovanni, in which you shall charge the drawer of the draft, the other entry in the account of your correspondent at Geneva, crediting Mr. Giovanni with that 100 ducats paid through a draft. This is the method that the bankers of all the world keep so that their transaction may appear clear; therefore you will have to take some trouble on your part and try to enter everything in its own place with great care.

CHAPTER 25.

ANOTHER ACCOUNT WHICH IS USUALLY KEPT IN THE LEDGER, CALLED INCOME AND EXPENSES, FOR WHICH OFTEN A SEPARATE BOOK IS USED, AND WHY.

There are some who, in their books, are accustomed to keep an account called Income and Expenses (*Entrata e uscita*), in which they enter extraordinary things, or any other thing that they deem proper; others keep an account called extraordinary expenses and in it they record gifts, which they receive or give. They keep it as a credit and debit account, and then at the end of the year they ascertain the remainder (*resto*) which is either a profit or a loss and transfer it to capital as you will understand when we talk about the balance. But really the account we have called "'household expenses" is sufficient for all this unless someone should like to keep a separate account for his own curiosity, but it would be of no great value because things should be arranged as briefly as possible. In other places it is customary to keep the income and expense account in a separate book which is balanced when they balance the authenticated books and all other affairs. This custom is not to be criticized but it requires more work.

CHAPTER 26.

HOW ENTRIES SHOULD BE MADE IN MERCANTILE BOOKS RELATIVE TO TRIPS WHICH YOU CONDUCT YOURSELF OR YOU ENTRUST TO OTHER PEOPLE, AND THE TWO LEDGERS RESULTING THEREFROM.

Trips are made usually in two ways, either personally or through somebody else; therefore two are the ways to keep their accounts and the book always ought to be in duplicate whether the trip is made by you personally or it is in charge of somebody else. One ledger is kept at home and the other one is taken along and kept on the trip. If you conduct the trip yourself, for the sake of order and system, you must take a new inventory also a small Ledger and small Journal among the things you take with you and follow the instruction above given. If you sell or buy or exchange, you must charge and credit according to the facts, persons, goods, cash, traveling capital, traveling profit and loss, etc. This is the best way, no matter what other people may say. You might keep an account with the mercantile house which furnishes you with the goods which you take on the trip. In this case you shall credit the said house in your little Ledger and charge the different goods one by one. In this way you would open your mercantile house accounts, capital account, etc., as in your main books, and coming back safe and sound you would return to the mercantile house either other goods in exchange for those that you took or money, and you would close the accounts with the entering in your big Ledger the respective profit or loss item. In this way your business will be clear. If, however, you entrust the trip to some other party, then you should charge this party with all the goods that you entrust with him, saying: Per trip entrusted to so and so, etc., and you should keep an account with him, as if he were one of your customers, for all goods and moneys, keeping separate accounts, etc., and he on his part will set up a little Ledger in which he makes you creditor for everything. When lie comes back he will balance with you; and if your traveling salesman were in fetters... [10]

CHAPTER 27.

ANOTHER WELL-KNOWN ACCOUNT NAMED PROFIT AND LOSS, OR PROFIT AND DEFICIT. HOW IT SHOULD BE KEPT IN THE LEDGER AND WHY IT IS NOT KEPT IN THE JOURNAL AS THE OTHER ACCOUNTS.

After the other accounts, there must follow one which is named variously, according to different localities, Favor and Damage (*Pro a Danno*), or Profit and Damage (*Utile a Danno*), or Increase and Deficit (*Avanzi e Desavanzi*). Into this other accounts in the Ledger have their remainders, as we will show when we speak of the trial balance. You should not put these entries in the Journal, but only in the Ledger, as they originate from overs or shorts in the debits and credits, and not from actual transactions. You shall open the account this way:

Profit and Loss debit (*dee dare*—shall give), and Profit and Loss credit (*dee havere*—shall have).

---

[10] Geijsbeek adds in parentheses: "sentence remains unfinished in the original."

That is, if you had sustained a loss in a special line of merchandise and in this account in your Ledger would show less in the credit than the debit, then you will add the difference (saldo) to the credit so as to make it balance, and you shall enter as follows:

Credit (*dee havere*—shall have), per Profit and Loss, so much, which I enter here in order to balance on account of Joss sustained—and so on, and you will mark the page of the Profit and Loss account where you write down the entry. Then you go to the Profit and Loss account and in the debit column you shall enter as follows:

Profit and Loss debit (*dee dare*—shall give), on this day, to such and such loss sustained, so much—which has been entered in the credit of said merchandise account in order to balance it at page so and so. If the account of this special merchandise would show a profit instead of loss— that is, more in the credit than in the debit—then you will proceed in the opposite way. The same you shall do one by one for all accounts with merchandise or different things, whether they show good or bad results, so that your Ledger always shows the accounts in balance—that is, as much In the debit as in the credit. This is the condition the Ledger will be in if it is correct, as I will explain to you when I am talking of the balance. In this way you will see at a glance whether you are gaining or losing, and how much. And this account must then be transferred for its closing (*saldo*) into the capital account, which is always the last in all the ledgers and is consequently the receptacle of all other accounts, as you will understand.

CHAPTER 28.

HOW FULL ACCOUNTS IN THE LEDGER SHOULD BE
CARRIED FORWARD AND THE PLACE TO WHICH THEY MUST
BE TRANSFERRED SO THAT NO CROOKEDNESS CAN BE
PRACTICED IN THE LEDGER.

You should know that when an account has been filled
out, either in the debit or in the credit, and you cannot make
any more entries in the space reserved for such an account,
you must at once carry this account forward to a page after
all your other accounts, so that there is no space left in the
Ledger between this transferred account and the last of the
other accounts. Otherwise it would be considered a fraud. It
must be carried forward in the manner which we have given
above when writing about the balancing of profit and loss.
In making the transfers, you should make entries on the
debit and credit sides only, without making any entry in the
Journal. Transfers are not made in the Journal; still, if you
so desired, you might do that and it would be all right; but it
Is not necessary, because it would be that much more
trouble without any necessity. All that need be done is to
increase the smaller quantity—that Is, if the account shows
more in the debit than in the credit, you ought to add the
difference to the credit. I will give you, now, an example of
one of these transfers:

Let us suppose that Martino has had a long account with
you of several transactions, so that his account should be
transferred from ledger [original] page 30. Suppose further
that the last account of your book Is at [original] page 60,
and is at the top of said page, so that on the same page there
is space enough to transfer the Martino account. Suppose
that there is on debit side, L 80, S 15, G 15, P 24; and the
credit shows that he has given you, L 72, S 9, G 3, P 17.

Deducting the credit from the debit, there is a remainder (*resta*) of: L 8, S 6, G 5, P 7. This is the amount that you should bring forward to the debit side of the new page, and on the old page you must add the same amount In the credit column to make it balance, saying as follows:

On such and such day, etc., per himself, I bring forward (*porta avanti*) this amount to the debit side as a remainder (resta), and the same amount I enter here per closing (saldo), that is: L 8, S 6, G 5, P 7. see at [original] page 60:

L... , S... , G... , P...

And you shall cancel the account both on the debit and credit side with a diagonal line. After that, you will go to [original] page 60 and shall enter in the debit column the said remainder, always writing down at the top of the page the year, if none already has been mentioned, as has been said above. You shall enter there as follows:

Martino debit on such and such day per himself, as per remainder (*resta*) taken from the page of his old account and therein entered per closing (*saldo*), see [original] page 30: L8, S6, G5, P7.

This is the way for you to proceed with all accounts that you should transfer: Place them, as I have told you, without leaving any space in between. The accounts should be opened in the order in which they originate in such place and at such time, so that nobody can speak evil of you.

CHAPTER 29.

HOW TO CHANGE THE YEAR IN THE LEDGER BETWEEN TWO SUCCESSIVE ENTRIES IN CASE THE BOOKS ARE NOT CLOSED EVERY YEAR.

It might be that you must change the year in your ledger accounts before you balance it. In this case, you should write the year in the margin before the first entry of the new year, as has been previously said at Chapter 15; all the following entries should be understood as having occurred during that year.

But it is always good to close the books each year, especially if you are In partnership with others. The proverb says: Frequent accounting makes for long friendship. Thus you will do in similar cases.

CHAPTER 30.

HOW AN ABSTRACT OR STATEMENT OF AN ACCOUNT SHOULD BE MADE TO A DEBTOR WHO MIGHT REQUEST IT, OR FOR YOUR EMPLOYER IN CASE YOU ARE MANAGER OR COMMISSIONER OF THE ADMINISTRATION OF HIS PROPERTY.

In addition, you must know how to make an abstract or a statement of an account if your debtor requests it. This is a favor that cannot be refused, especially if your debtor has had an account with you for years or months, etc. In this case you should go away back to the time when you began to have transactions with him, or back to the time from which he desires to have his statement, in case you have had previous settlements. And you should do this willingly. You should copy all his account on a sheet of paper large enough to contain it all. If it should not be large enough, you will draw a balance at the end of the page and shall carry the latter. In debit or credit, forward to the other side of the sheet, as I told you at Chapter 28. And so on, until the end of the account, and at the end you must reduce the whole account to the net remainder In a single entry in debit or credit, according to the facts. These statements must be made out very carefully.

The following is the way you have to proceed in adjusting your own business with the business of your employer. But if you should act for others as an agent or commissioner, then you will make out a statement for your employer just as it appears in the ledger, crediting yourself from time to time with your commissions according to your agreements. Then at the end you shall charge yourself with the net remainder, or you shall credit yourself if you had to put in any money of your own. Your employer will then go through this statement, compare it with his own book, and if he finds it correct, he will like you better and trust you more. For this reason, of all the things that he gave or sent you, you should with your own handwriting keep an orderly account when you receive them. Observe this carefully. On the contrary, if you are the employer, you may have your managers or commissioners make out these statements for you. But before these statements are delivered they ought to be compared carefully with each entry in the Ledger, Journal and Memorandum Book, or with any other paper relative thereto, so that no mistake could be made between the parties.

CHAPTER 31.

HOW TO TAKE OUT ONE OR MORE ENTRIES WHICH BY MISTAKE YOU MIGHT HAVE ENTERED IN A DIFFERENT PLACE FROM THE RIGHT ONE. WHICH MAY HAPPEN THROUGH ABSENTMINDEDNESS.

The good bookkeeper should also know how to take out— or as they call it in Florence "*stornare*"—an entry which by mistake you might have written down in the wrong place as, for instance, if you had entered it as a debit instead of a credit entry; or when you have to enter it in the account of Mr. Martino and you put it in the account of Mr. Giovanni.

For at times you cannot be so diligent that you are unable to make mistakes. The proverb says: He who does nothing, makes no mistakes: he who makes no mistakes, learns nothing.

And you shall correct this entry as follows: If you had placed this entry in the debit column while you should have put it in the credit column, in order to correct this, you shall make another entry opposite this one in the credit for the same amount. And you shall say thus : On such and such day for the amount which has been entered opposite here under the debit and should have been put in the credit, see page, etc., and you shall write down in the column of figures: L... S... G... P... which you wrote down by mistake in the other column. In front of these two entries you shall mark a cross or any other mark so that when you make out an abstract or statement of the account you should leave these entries out. After you have made this correction it is just as if you had written nothing in the debit column. You then make the entry in the credit column as it should have been and everything will be as it should have been.

CHAPTER 32.

HOW THE BALANCE OF THE LEDGER IS MADE AND HOW THE ACCOUNTS OF AN OLD LEDGER ARE TRANSFERRED TO A NEW ONE.

After all we have said you must know now how to carry forward the accounts from one Ledger to another if you want to have a new Ledger for the reason that the old one is all filled up or because another year begins, as is customary in the best known places, especially at Milan where the big merchants renew every year their Ledgers.

This operation, together with the operations of which we will speak, is called the balancing (*bilancio*) of the Ledger, and if you want to do this well you shall do it with great diligence and order. That is, first you shall get a helper as you could hardly do it alone. You give him the Journal for greater precaution and you shall keep the Ledger. Then you tell him, beginning with the first entry in the Journal, to call the numbers of the pages of your Ledger where that entry has been made, first in debit and then in credit. Accordingly in turn you shall obey him and shall always find the page in the Ledger that he calls and you shall ask him what kind of an entry it is, that is, for what and for whom, and you shall look at the pages to which he refers to see if you find that item and that account. If the amount is the same, call it out. If you find it there the same as in the journal, check it (*lanzarala*—mark it with a lance A or V) or dot it (*pontarala*), or any proper mark over the lire mark, or in some other place, so that you can readily see it. You ask your helper to make a similar mark or check—as we are used to call it in some places—in the Journal at the same entry. Care must be taken that no entry will be dotted (*pontata*) either by you without him, or by him without you, as great mistakes might be made otherwise, for once the entry is dotted it means that it is correct. The same is done in making out statements of accounts for your debtors before you deliver them. They should have been compared with the Ledger and Journal, or with any other writing in which the entries of the transaction have been recorded, as we have said at Chapter 30.

After you have proceeded in this way through all the accounts of the Ledger and Journal and found that the two books correspond in debit and credit. It will mean that all the accounts are correct and the entries entered correctly. Take care that your helper shall mark each entry in the Journal with two dots or little lances; In the ledger you mark down only one for each entry because you know that for each entry in the Journal there are two made in the Ledger, therefore, the two dots or lances.

In making this balance it is good if you mark in the Journal two dots or lances under the lire, one under the other. This will mean that the entry is correct in debit and credit in the Ledger. Some use these marks in the Journal: They put a mark before the per for the debit and after the lire for the credit. Any way both customs are good, however, one single mark in the Journal might be enough, that is, only the debit mark, because you can then mark yourself the credit side on the page of the Ledger where that entry is as this page is mentioned in the debit entry in your ledger. It will then not be necessary for your helper to call to you this credit page. So that by comparing only the debit side with him you could yourself check the credit side. But it would be more convenient for you if you proceed with your helper in the manner above said.

After you have finished checking off the Journal, if you find in the Ledger some account or entry which has not been checked off in debit or credit, this would indicate that there has been some mistake in the Ledger, that is, that that entry is superfluous whether in the debit or credit, and you shall correct this error by making an entry for the same amount in the opposite side—that is, if the superfluous entry was in the debit, you make an entry on the credit side, or *vice versa*. And how you should proceed to correct the error I have told you in the preceding chapter. The same would be done in case your helper finds some entry which your ledger did not show whether in the debit or credit column, which also would indicate an error in the ledger and should be corrected in a different way. That is, you should make that entry or open that account in the debit or credit, mentioning the different dates, as the entry would be made later than it should have been. A good bookkeeper should always mention why such differences arise, so that the books are above suspicion; thus the notary public in his instruments need not mention what has been added or omitted. Thus the good bookkeeper must act so that the mercantile reputation be kept up.

But if the said entry should have been entered on only one side, debit or credit, then it would be sufficient for you to put it where it is missing, mentioning how it happened through mistake, etc. So you will go on through all your accounts and, if they agree, you know that your Ledger is right and well kept.

You must know that there may be found in the Ledger some entries which are not in the Journal and cannot be found in the Journal. These are the difference between the debit and credit placed there to close (*per saldi*) the different accounts when they are carried forward, as we have said in Chapter 28. Of these balances or remainders, you will find their correlative entries in the Ledger, whether in debit or credit, on the page indicated in these accounts. When you find each correlative entry in its proper place, you may conclude that your Ledger is in proper order.

What we have said so far about comparing the Ledger with the Journal, should be observed also in comparing the memorandum book or scrap book with the Journal, day by day, if you use the memorandum book, in the manner I spoke about at the beginning of this treatise. If you have other books, you should do the same. The last book to be compared should be the Ledger, the next to the last the Journal.

CHAPTER 33.

HOW THE TRANSACTIONS WHICH MIGHT OCCUR WHILE YOU BALANCE YOUR BOOKS SHOULD BE RECORDED. AND HOW IN THE OLD BOOKS NO ENTRY SHOULD BE MADE OR CHANGED DURING THAT TIME, AND REASONS WHY.

After you have regularly done and observed all these things, see that no new entry is made in any book which comes before the Ledger—that is, in the memorandum book and Journal—because the equalizing or closing (*el saldo*) of all the books should be understood to take place on the same day. But if, while you are balancing you books, some transactions should occur, you shall enter them in the new books to which you intend to carry forward the old ones— that is, in the memorandum book or Journal, but not in the Ledger, until you have carried forward all the different accounts of the old Ledger. If you have not yet a new set of books, then you will record these transactions and their respective explanations on a separate sheet of paper until the books are ready. When the new books are ready, you enter them in these books which shall bear new marks—that is, if the old ones that you are balancing now were marked with a cross, then you should mark these new ones with the capital letter A.

CHAPTER 34.

HOW ALL THE ACCOUNTS OF THE OLD LEDGER SHOULD BE CLOSED AND WHY. ABOUT THE GRAND TOTALS OF THE DEBITS AND CREDITS, WHICH IS THE PREPARATION OF THE TRIAL BALANCE.

After you have done this carefully, you shall close your Ledger accounts in this way: You should commence first with cash account, then the different debtors, then the merchandise, and then your customers. Transfer the remainders in Ledger A, that is, in the new Ledger. You should not, as I have said above, transfer the remainders in the new Journal.

You shall add all the different entries in debit and in credit, always adding to the smaller side the difference, as I have told you above when explaining the carrying forward of the remainder. These two accounts are practically the same thing ; the only difference is that in the first case the remainder was carried forward to another page of the same Ledger, while in this instance it is carried forward from one Ledger to another. While in the first instance you would mark down the new page of the same Ledger, in this case you mark down the page of the new Ledger; making the transfer from one ledger to another, any account should appear only once in each ledger. This is a peculiarity of the last entry of the accounts of the Ledgers.

In making the transfer, you should proceed as follows : Let us suppose that the account of Mr. Martino has a debit remainder (*resto*) in your "Cross" Ledger at [original] page 60 of   L 12, S. 15, G 10. P. 26, and you want to transfer it to Ledger A at [original] page 8 in debit; in the "Cross" Ledger you have to add to the credit column and you shall put the following at the end of all the other entries: On such and such day—putting down always the same day in which you do the balancing (*bilancio*)—per himself as posted to Ledger A to the debit, per remainder (*resto*), which amount I add here in order to close (*saldo*)— value ; see [original] page 8:   L 12, S 15, G 10, P 26.

And then you shall cancel the account in the debit and credit diagonally, as I have told you in talking about the bringing forward of the accounts. Then put down the total of all the entries, in the debit as well as in the credit, so that the eye can see at a glance that it is all even. You shall also write down at the new page in Ledger A, in the debit column, as follows: First you put down at the top of the page the year, and you put the day in front of the place where you make the entry for the reason mentioned in Chapter 15, then you say, Mr. Martino so and so, debit *(dee dare*—shall give) on such and such day per himself as per remainder (*resto*) carried from "Cross" Ledger, which has been added in the credit column in order to close (*saldo*), see [original] page 60, value: L 12, S 15, Q 10, P 26.

Thus you will proceed with all the accounts of the Gross Ledger which you want to transfer to Ledger A: cash account, capital account, merchandise, personal property, real property, debtors, creditors, public officers, brokers, public weighmen, etc., with whom we have sometimes very long accounts. But as to those accounts which you should not care to transfer to Ledger A, as, for instance, your own personal accounts of which you are not obliged to give an account to another, as, for instance, small mercantile expenses, household expenses, income and expenses and all extraordinary expenses—rentals, *pescioni, feudi* or *livelli*, etc. AU these accounts should be closed (*saldore*) in the Cross Ledger into the favor and damage account, or increase and deficit, or profit and damage account, as it is sometimes called. You shall enter them in the debit column, as it is rare that these expense accounts should show anything in the credit side. As I often have told you, add the difference to the column, either debit or credit, which shows a smaller total, saying: Per profit and loss in this account, see page, etc. By doing so, you shall have closed (*saldore*) all these different accounts in the profit and loss account through which then, by adding all the debit and all the credit entries, you will be able to know what is your gain or loss, for with this balance all entries are equalized; the things that had to be deducted were deducted, and the things that had to be added were added proportionately in their respective places. If this account shows more in the debit than in the credit, that means that you have lost that much in your business since you began. If the credit is more than the debit, that means that in the same period of time you have gained.

After you know by the closing (*saldorai*) of this account what your profit or loss is, then you shall close this account into the capital account in which, at the beginning of your management of your business, you entered the inventory of all your worldly goods. You shall close the account in this way: If the losses are in excess—from which state of affairs may God keep every one who really lives as a good Christian—then you have to add to the credit in the usual manner, saying: On such and such day, Per capital on account of losses in this account, see page so and so, value, etc. Then you shall cancel the account with a diagonal line in debit and credit, and put in the total amount of all the debit entries, as well as of the credit entries, which should be equal. And then in the capital account, you shall write in the debit column: Capital debit (*dee dare*—shall give) on such and such day, per profit and loss account on account of losses as marked down in the credit column of said account in order to close (*per saldo*), value, etc.:

L… , S… , G… , P…

If instead there should be a profit, which will happen when the profit and loss account would show more in the credit than in the debit, then you should add the difference to the debit side to make the equalization, referring to the capital account and respective page. You should credit the same amount to the capital account, making the entry on the credit side where all the other goods of yours have been entered, personal or real. Therefore, from the capital account, which always must be the last account in the entire Ledger, you may always learn what your fortune is, by adding together all the debits and all the credits, which you have transferred in Ledger A.

Then this capital account should be closed and carried forward with the other accounts to Ledger A, either in total or entry by entry. You can do either way, but it is customary to transfer only the total amount, so that the entire value of your inventory (*inventario*) is shown at a glance. Don't forget to number the pages, after which you will enter all the different accounts in the alphabet of Ledger A, each at its own place, as I have said at Chapter 5, so that you may find very easily the account you want. In this way the entire first Ledger, and with it the Journal and memorandum book, are closed and closed up.

In order that it may be clearer that the books were correct before the said closing, you shall summarize on a sheet of paper all the debit totals that appear in the Cross Ledger and place them at the left, then you shall write down all the credit totals at the right. Of all these debit totals you make one sum total which is called grand total (*summa summarum*) , and likewise you shall make a sum total of all the credit totals, which is also called grand total (*summa summarum*) . The first is the grand total of the debits, and the second is the grand total of the credits. Now, if these two grand totals are equal—that is, if one is just as much as the other—that is, if those of the debit and those of the credit are alike—then you shall conclude that your Ledger was very well kept and closed, for the reason that I gave you in Chapter 14. But if one of the grand totals is bigger than the other, that would indicate a mistake in your Ledger, which mistake you will have to look for diligently with the industry and the intelligence God gave you and with the help of what you have learned. This part of the work, as we said at the beginning, is highly necessary to the good merchant, for, if you are not a good bookkeeper in your business, you will go on groping like a blind man and may meet great losses.

Therefore, take good care and make all efforts to be a good bookkeeper, such as I have shown you fully in this sublime work how to become one. I have given you all the rules and indicated the places where everything can be found, in the table of contents which I have placed at the beginning of this work.

Of all the things thus far treated, as I promised you in Chapter 12, I will now give you a summary of the most essential things for your own recollection, which no doubt will be very useful to you.

And remember to pray God for me so that to His praise and glory I may always go on doing good.

CHAPTER 35.

HOW AND IN WHAT ORDER PAPERS SHOULD BE KEPT.
SUCH AS MANUSCRIPTS, FAMILY LETTERS, POLICIES,
PROCESSES, JUDGMENTS AND OTHER INSTRUMENTS OF
WRITING AND THE RECORD BOOK OF IMPORTANT LETTERS.

Here follow the manner and rules for keeping documents and manuscripts, such as papers relative to payments made, receipts for drafts, or gifts of merchandise, confidential letters, which things are very important for merchants and, if they are lost, may cause great danger.

First, we shall talk of confidential letters which you may write to or receive from your customers. You should always keep these in a little desk until the end of the month. At the end of the month tie them together in a bunch and put them away and write on the outside of each the date of receipt and the date of reply, and do this month by month, then, at the end of the year, of all these papers make one big bundle and write on it the year, and put it away. Any time you need a letter, go to these bundles.

Keep in your desk pouches in which to place the letters that your friends may give you to be sent away with your own letters. If the letter should be .sent to Rome, put it in the Rome pouch, and if to Florence, put it in the Florence pouch, etc. And then when you send your messenger, put these letters with yours and send them to your correspondent in that particular town. To be of service is always a good thing, and it is customary also to give a gratuity for that good service.

You should have several little compartments, or little bags, as many as there are places or cities in which you do business, as, for instance, Rome, Florence, Naples, Milan, Genoa, Lyon, London, Bruges, and on each little bag you shall write its proper name—that is, you will write on one "Rome," on another "Florence," etc., and in these bags you shall put the letters that somebody might send you to be forwarded to those places.

When you have answered a letter and sent the answer away, you shall mention on the outside of the said letter the answer, by whom you sent it and the day, just as you did when you received the letter.

As to the day, you shall never forget to mark it in any of your transactions, whether small or large, and especially in writing letters in which these things must be mentioned, namely: the year, the day, the lace, and your name. It is customary to put the name at the end of the right side in a corner. It is customary among merchants to write the year and the day and the place at the top at the beginning of the letter. But first, like a good Christian, you shall always remember to write down the glorious name of our Savior— that is, the name of Jesus, or in its place the sign of the Holy Cross, in whose name our transactions must always be made, and you shall do as follows: Cross 1494. On this 17th day of April in Venice.

And then go on with what you want to say—that is, "My very dear," etc. But the students and other people, like the monks or priests, etc., who are not in business, are used to writing the day and year at the end after writing the letter. The merchants are accustomed to put at the top as we have said. If you should do otherwise and not write the day, there will be confusion and you will be made fun of because we say the letter which does not bear the day was written during the night, and the letter which does not bear the place we say that it was written in the other world, not in this one; and besides the fun made of you, there would be vexations, which is worse, as I have said.

After you have sent your answer away, you put your letter in its proper place; and what we have said of one letter will apply to all the other letters. It must be observed that when the letters you send away are of importance, you should first make a record of them in a book which is kept for this special purpose. In this book the letter should be copied, word for word, if it is of great importance—as, for instance, the letters of exchange, or letters of goods sent, etc., otherwise only a record of the substantial part should be made similarly as we do in the memorandum book, saying: On this day, etc., we have written to so and so, etc., and we send him the following things, etc., as per his letter of such and such date he requested or gave commission for, etc., which letter we have placed in such and such pouch.

After you have sealed the letter on the outside and addressed it, it is the custom of many to mark on the outside your special mark, so that they may know that it is correspondence of a merchant, because great attention is given to merchants, for they are the ones, as we said at the beginning of this treatise, who support our republics.

For this purpose, the Most Reverend Cardinals do likewise, by writing their name on the outside of their correspondence so that nobody could claim as an excuse that he did not know from whom it was. The correspondence of the Holy Father remains open so that its contents may be known, like bulls, privileges, etc., although for things which are more personal or confidential the seal representing the Fisherman (*Pescatore*—St. Peter) is used to seal them.

All these letters, then, month by month, year by year, you shall put together in a bundle and you will keep them in an orderly way in a chest, wardrobe or cupboard. As you receive them during the day, put them aside in the same order, so that if necessary you might find them more easily;

and I won't talk any longer about this, as I know that you have understood it.

You shall keep in a more secret place, as private boxes and chests, all manuscripts of your debtors who have not paid you, as I said in Chapter 17. Likewise keep the receipts in a safe place for any emergency. But when you should pay others, have the other party write the receipt in a receipt book, as I told you at the beginning, so that a receipt cannot be easily lost or go astray.

You shall do the same as to important writing, as, for instance, memoranda of the brokers, or of merchants, or of weighmen, or relative to goods placed in or taken out of the custom house, either land or sea custom houses, and judgments or decrees of the consuls or of other public officials, or all kinds of notarial instruments written on parchments which ought to be kept in a place apart. The same should be said of the copies of instruments and papers of attorneys or counselors at law relative to lawsuits.

It is also wise to have a separate book for memoranda, which we call memoranda book, in which day by day you shall keep a record of the things that you might be afraid of forgetting and, if you forget them, may prove to be dangerous to you. Every day, the last thing in the evening, just before going to bed, you shall glance over this book to see whether everything which should have been done has been done, etc., and you shall cancel with your pen the things that have been don(>, and in this book you shall make a record of the things that you have lent to your neighbor or friend for one or two days, as, for instance, store vases, caldrons, or any other thing.

These rules, and the other very useful rules of which I have spoken before, you shall follow and, according to the localities and times, you shall be more or less particular, adding or omitting as it seems best to you, because it is impossible to give rules for every little thing in the mercantile business, as we have already said. The proverb says that we need more bridges to make a merchant than a doctor of laws can make.

If you understand well all the things that I have spoken of so far, I am sure you with your intelligence will carry on your business well.

CHAPTER 36.

SUMMARY OF THE RULES AND WAYS FOR KEEPING A LEDGER.

All the creditors must appear in the Ledger at the right hand side, and all the debtors at the left.

All entries made in the ledger have to be double entries—that is, if you make one creditor, you must make some one debtor.

Each debit (shall give—d*ee dare*) and credit (shall have —*dee havere*) entry must contain three things, namely: the day, the amount and the reason for the entry.

The last name in the entry of the debit (in the Ledger) must be the first name in the entry of the credit. On the same day that you make the debit entry, you should make the credit entry.

By a trial balance (*bilancio*) of the Ledger we mean a sheet of paper folded lengthwise in the middle, on which we write down all the creditors of the Ledger at the right side and the debtors at the left side. We see whether the total of the debits is equal to that of the credits, and if so, the Ledger is in order.

The trial balance of the Ledger should be equal—that is, the total of the credits—I do not say creditors—should be equal to the total of the debits—I do not say debtors. If they were not equal there would be a mistake in the Ledger.

The cash account should always be a debtor or equal. If it were different, there would be a mistake in the ledger.

You must not and cannot make any one debtor in your book without permission or consent of the person that has to appear as debtor; if you should, that account would be considered false. Likewise you cannot add terms or conditions to a credit without permission and consent of the creditor. If you should, that statement would be untrue.

The values in the Ledger must be reckoned in one kind of money. In the explanation of the entries, you may name all sorts of money, either *ducats*, or *lire*, or *Florence*, or gold *scudi*, or anything else; but in writing the amount in the column, you should always use the same kind of money throughout—that is, the money that you reckon by at the beginning should be the same all through the Ledger.

The debit or credit entries of the cash account may be shortened, if you desire, by not giving the reason for the entry ; you may simply say from so and so, for so and so, because the reason for the entry is stated in the opposite entry.

If a new account should be opened, you must use a new page and must not go back even if there was room enough to place the new account. You should not write backward, but always forward—that is, go forward as the days go, which never come back. If you do otherwise, the book would be untrue.

If you should make an entry in the Ledger by mistake which should not have been made, as it happens at times through absentmindedness, and if you wanted to correct it, you shall do as follows: Mark with a cross or with an "H" that special entry, and then make an entry on the opposite side under the same account. That is, if the erroneous entry was on the credit side—say, for instance, for L 50, S 10, D 6—you make an entry in the debit side, saying: Debit (*dee dare*) L 50, S 10, D 6, for the opposite entry cross marked which is hereby corrected, because it was put in through a mistake and should not have been made. Then mark with a cross this new entry. This is all.

When the spaces given to any particular account are all filled so that no more entries can be made and you want to carry forward that account, do in this way : Figure out the remainder of the said account—that is, whether it is debit or credit remainder. Now let us say that there is a credit remainder of L 20, S 4, D 2. You should write on the opposite side, without mentioning any date, as follows : Debit L 28, S 4, D 2, per remainder (*per resto*) of this account carried forward in the credit at page so and so. And it is done. The said entry is to be marked in the margin so, namely: Ro, which means "*resto*" (remainder), but this does not mean that it is a true debit entry although it is on the debit side. It is rather the credit which is transferred through the debit side. Now you must turn the pages and keep on turning them until you find a new page where you shall credit that account by naming the account and making a new entry without putting down any day. And you shall say in the following manner: So and so is credit (*dee havere*) L 28, S 4, D 2, per remainder (*per resto*) of account transferred from page so and so, and you should mark this entry in the margin by *Ro*, which means "*resto*" remainder, and that is done.

In the same way, as I have shown you, you shall proceed if the account has a debit remainder—that is, what you enter on the credit side you should transfer to the debit side.

When the ledger is all filled up, or old, and you want to transfer it into a new one, you proceed in the following manner: First you must see whether your old book bears a mark on its cover—for instance, an A. In this case you must mark the new Ledger in which you want to transfer the old one by B. because the books of the merchants go by order, one after the other, according to the letters of the alphabet. Then you have to take the trial balance of the old book and see that it is equal. From the trial balance sheet you must copy in the new Ledger all the creditors and debtors all in order just as they appear in the trial balance sheet, but make a separate account for each amount; and leave to each account all the space that you thin you may need. And in each debit account you shall say : Per so much as per debit remainder (*resta a dare*) in the old book marked A, at page so and so. And in each credit account you shall say: Per so much as per credit remainder (*resta a havere*) in the old book marked A, at page so and so. In this way you transfer the old Ledger into the new one. Now, in order to cancel the old book, you must cancel each account by making it balance, of which we have spoken—that is, if an account of the old Ledger shows a credit remainder as the trial balance would show you, you shall debit this account for the same amount, saying, so much remains in the credit of this account, carried forward in the credit in the new Ledger marked B, at page so and so. In this way you shall have closed the old Ledger and opened the new one for, as I have shown you how to do for a creditor, the same you shall do for a debtor, with this difference, that while you debit an account, which may show a credit remainder, you shall credit the account which may show a debit remainder. This is all.

THINGS WHICH SHOULD BE ENTERED IN THE BOOKS
OF THE MERCHANTS.

Of all the cash that you might have, if it is your own—
that is, that you might have earned at different times in the
past, or which might have been bequeathed to you by your
dead relatives or given you as a gift from some Prince, you
shall make yourself creditor (*crcditore te medesima*), and
make cash debitor. As to all jewelry or goods which might
be your own—that is, that you may have got through
business or that might have been left you through a will or
given to you as a present, you must value them in cash and
make as many accounts as there are things and make each
debitor by saying: For so many, etc., of which I find myself
possessed on this day, so many *denari*, posted credit entry
at such and such page; and then you make creditor your
account (*tuo conto*), that is yourself (*medesimo*) , with the
amount of each of these entries. But remember these entries
should not be for less than ten ducats each, as small things
of little value are not entered in the Ledger.

Of all the real property that you might own, as houses,
lands, stores, you make the cash debitor and estimate their
value at your discretion in cash, and you make creditor
yourself or your personal account (*tuo sopradette conto*).
Then you make debitor an account of that special property
by giving the value, as I have said above, and make yourself
creditor because, as I have told you, all entries must have
three things : The date, the value in cash, and the reason.

If you should buy merchandise or anything else for
cash, you should make a debtor of that special merchandise
or thing and like creditor cash, and if you should say, I
bought that merchandise for cash, but a bank will furnish
the cash, or a friend of mine will do so, I will answer you

that any way, you must make a debitor of that special merchandise; but where I told you to credit cash, you should, instead, credit that special bank, or that special friend who furnished the money.

If you should buy merchandise or anything else, partly for cash and partly on time, you shall make that special merchandise debitor, and make a creditor of the party from whom you bought it on time and under the conditions that you might have agreed upon ; as, for instance, one-third in cash and the rest in six months. After this you will have to make another entry—that is, make a debitor of the party from whom you bought it for the amount of the cash that you have given him for that one-third, and make creditor cash or the bank which might have paid that much for you.

If you should sell any merchandise or anything else, you should proceed as above with the exception that you should proceed in the opposite way—that is, where I told you that when you bought you should make the merchandise debitor, when you sell you will have to make your merchandise a creditor and charge the cash account if it is sold for cash, or charge the bank that might have promised the payment. And if you make a sale on time, you will have to charge the party to whom you sold it on time, and if you make the sale partly for cash and partly on time, you shall proceed as I have shown you in explaining about the buying.

If you should give merchandise in exchange, for instance, let us say I have sold 1,000 pounds of English wool in exchange for pepper—that is, for 2,000 pounds of pepper—I ask, how shall we make this entry in the Ledger ? You shall do as follows: Estimate what the value of the pepper is, at your discretion, in cash. Now let us say that you estimated 12 ducats per hundred; the 2,000 pounds would be worth 210 ducats. Therefore, you shall make the wool a creditor with 240 ducats, for which amount you have sold it. This is the manner that you should follow in all the trade entries. If you have received 2,000 pounds of pepper valued at 240 ducats, you shall make the pepper a debitor and say : Said pepper debtor on this day, see page, etc., etc.

If you should loan cash to some of your friends, you shall charge the friend to whom you have given it and credit cash. If you should borrow cash from some friend, you will have to debit cash and credit your friend.

If you have received 8 or 10 or 20 ducats in order to insure a ship or a galley, or anything else, you should credit the account "ship insurance," and explain all about it—how, when and where, and how much per cent.; and shall charge the cash account.

If anybody should send you any goods with instructions to sell them or exchange them on commission, I say that you have to charge in the Ledger that special merchandise belonging to so and so with the freight, or duty, or for storage, and credit the cash account. You shall credit the cash for all cash that you have to pay on account of goods: for instance, cash paid for transportation or duty, or brokerage, etc., and charge the account of that special goods for that which you have paid in money.

THINGS THAT SHOULD BE RECORDED IN A RECORD BOOK (*RECORDANZE*) OP THE MERCHANT.

All the house and store goods that you may find yourself possessed of—these should be put down in order— that is, all the things made of iron by itself, leaving space enough to make additions if necessary; also leaving room to mark in the margin the things that might be lost or sold or given as presents or spoiled. But I don't mean small things of little value.

Make a record of all the brass things separately, as I have said, and then a record of the tin things, and then the wooden things, and copper things, and then the silver things and gold things, always leaving enough space between each class so that you may add something if necessary, and to put down a memorandum of any object that might be missing.

All sureties or obligations or promises of payment that you might make for some friend, explaining clearly everything.

All goods or other things that might be left with you in custody, or that you might borrow from some friend, as well as all the things that other friends of yours might borrow from you.

All conditional transactions—that is, purchases and sales, as, for instance, a contract that you shall send me by the next ship coming from England, so many *cantara* of *woll di li mistri,* on condition that it is good; and when I receive it I will pay you so much per cantara or by the hundred, or otherwise; I will send you in exchange so many *cantara* of cotton.

All houses, lands, stores or jewels that you might rent at so many ducats and so many lire per year. And when you collect the rent, then that money should be entered in the Ledger, as I have told you.

If you should lend some jewels, silver or gold vase to some friend, say, for instance, for eight or fifteen days, things like this should not be entered in the Ledger, but should be recorded in this record book, because in a few days, you will get them back. In the same way, if somebody should lend you something like the things mentioned, you should not make any entry in the Ledger, but put down a little memorandum in the record book, because in a short time you will have to give it back.

How *Lire, Soldi, Denari and Picioli,* etc., should be written down as abbreviations.

Lire; Soldi; Denari; Picioli; Libbre; Once; Danarpesi; Grani; Carati; Ducati; Florin larghi.

HOW THE DEBIT (LEDGER) ENTRIES ARE MADE.		HOW THE CREDIT (LEDGER) ENTRIES ARE MADE.	
MCCCCLXXXXIII. Lodovico, son of Piero Forestani, shall give on the 14th day of November, 1493, L 44, S 1, D 8, for cash loaned, posted cash shall have at page 2:		MCCCCLXXXXIII. Lodovico, son of Piero Forestani, shall have, on Nov. 22, 1493, for L 20, S 4, D 2, for part payment. And for him Francesco, son of Antonio Cavalcanti, promised to pay it to us at our pleasure ; posted shall give at	
	L44, S 1, D 8	page 2:	L 20, S 4, D 2
And on the 18th ditto, L 18, S 11, D 6, which we promised to pay for him to Martino, son of Piero Foraboschi at his pleasure, posted said shall have at page 2:		Cash in hands of Simone, son of Alessio Bombeni, shall have, on Nov. 14, 1493, for L 44, S 1, D 8, from Lodovico Pietro Forestani, L 44, S 1, D 8 ; and on Nov. 22, 1493, L 18, S 11, D 6, to Martino, son of Piero Forbaschi,	
	L18, S ll, D6	page 2:	L 18, S 11, D 6

HOW THE DEBIT (LEDGER) ENTRIES ARE MADE. (CONTINUED)		HOW THE CREDIT (LEDGER) ENTRIES ARE MADE. (CONTINUED)	
Martino, son of Piero Foraboschi, shall give on Nov. 20, 1493, for L 18, S 11, D 6, taken by him in cash, posted Cash at page 2:		Martino, son of Piero Foraboschi, shall have on Nov. 18, 1493, for L18, Sll, D6, which we promised to pay him at his pleasure for Lodovico, son of Pietro Forestani ; posted	
	L 18, S 11, D 6	shall give entry at p. 8:	L18, Sll, D6
Francesco, son of Antonio Cavalcanti, shall give, on Nov. 12, 1493, L20, S4, D 2, which he promised to pay to us at our pleasure for Lodovico, son of Pietro Forestani ; page 2:	L 20, S 4, D 2	Francesco, son of Antonio Cavalcanti, shall have on Nov. 14, 1493, for L 62, S 13, D 6, which he brought himself in cash; posted cash shall give at page 2:	L 62, S 13, D 6 81

APPENDIX

Introduction to John B. Geijsbeek's (1914)
"Ancient Double Entry–Bookkeeping"

By Page Lawrence, C.P.A.

Nearly all historians, when tracing the growth of an art or science from mere empiricism to the establishment of recognized principles, are confronted with an apparent insurmountable gap or complete silence during the period known in history as the Dark Ages.

Archaeological and historical researches have convinced this civilization that in Ancient Babylon, Greece and Rome there was a high state of civilization—both industrial and social.

Today we may study Aristotle's politics with great profit in our attempts to understand the political and economic conditions confronting this generation. An acquaintance with the Greek philosophers is essential in understanding our present philosophical thought.

It would seem that, since we find so much help in consulting these ancient writers in an attempt to solve the political problems of today which are presented by this complex civilization, in a large measure at least our mentors must have been confronted with the same economic and industrial difficulties that we are attempting to solve now as accountants.

One is convinced that the ancient writers on political economy and commerce were closely allied with the scribes or accountants who recorded the business transactions of those days. This allegiance seems to have been lost after the

Roman supremacy (and the consequent growth and spread of commerce), and it is only within recent years that the modern economist and accountant has acknowledged that a truer understanding of modern commerce can be had with cooperation and that the two sciences (economics and accounting) are finding so much in common that each is dependent upon the other for a full understanding of modern business conditions.

Mr. John P. Young, Editor of the San Francisco Chronicle, ably presented accounting in antiquity before the convention of the American Association of Public Accountants at San Francisco (Year Book 1911, page 153). He showed that Rome in Cicero's time was dependent upon the independent verification of accounts and statements thereof by one skilled in accountancy. The familiarity with which he mentions the accountant would seem to indicate that his place in the Roman social organization was well established.

However, after the recorded utterances of Cicero the historian finds in the pages of history no further mention of those individuals acknowledged to be skilled in accounts, which we are pleased to call accountants, until the writings of Pacioli in 1494 and Stevin in 1604.

It seems especially appropriate that one so greatly interested as the author in that work dear to the hearts of all progressive accountants, and who has done so much to place the education of the accountant on equal footing with that of law or medicine, should be the first of modern times to translate this first recorded book of the principles of debit and credit into the English language.

It is a significant fact that the rules and principles elucidated by Pacioli are contained in a book given over to mathematics. One cannot help but believe that the derivation of double-entry bookkeeping is an explanation of

the algebraic equation used with such skill by the ancient Greek mathematicians, applied
practically to the scientific recording of business transactions for, just as in algebra, the equation once established cannot be changed but by the addition of positive or negative quantities.

This work will give an added assurance that the apparently empirical rules of commerce are based upon an ancient scientific and mathematical foundation, to those who have attempted to instill into the commercial mind the idea that accountancy is a science, the prime requisite of a mastery of which is a thorough education in the theory of economics and allied sciences supplemented by practical experimentation in the application of formulae to practical business situations.

The accountant has to correct constantly, or at least modify, the attitude of the business man toward matters which are his dearest heirlooms handed down from the days of the Ancient Guild system, i. e., that the only way to learn how to do business is to do it along the rule-of-thumb method communicated from father to son by word of mouth.

Accountants, who remember the dearth of accountancy literature in this country up to a few short years ago, are dumbfounded at the mass of accountancy publications which are constantly flooding the market at this time. While I believe that the profession of accountancy as a whole recognizes the inestimable value of these publications, one cannot help but think in perusing their pages that they are largely influenced by the empirical methods of general business, rather than based on scientific principles. In other words, on "how" but never "why."

We are wont to look in vain through mazes of descriptions, forms and precedence of some particular business enterprise for a principle of accountancy which can be applied to the specific difficulty we have in hand. It should be the aim of some of the brilliant members of the profession of accountancy to take the great mass of historical records which have been published in the last few years of how this or that business should be kept and, with the aid of recognized authorities on economics, codify, with quotation of their source, the scattered and ill defined principles of accountancy for the benefit of accountancy education, and to this end no better examples of axiomatic principles can be had than in the books of Pacioli, Pietra and Stevin.

The author, recognizing from his experience as an educator in accountancy (coming as he did from Holland some twenty years ago without knowledge of American commercial practices or language) the lack of clearly expressed principles in accountancy, commenced researches which have finally culminated in this published translation in English of the first known writings on the subject of double entry bookkeeping.

At every turn, in the preachment of the scientific principles of his profession to the commercial mind, in his successful efforts for the passage of the Certified Public Accounts law in Colorado, then in his work as secretary of the first examining board in that state, in his labors as Dean of the School of Commerce, Accounts and Finance of The University of Denver, and as an instructor on practical and theoretical accountancy subjects and, finally as Chairman of the Educational Committee of The American Association of Public Accountants, the author has ever been confronted with the dearth of practical exemplification, historical or otherwise, of the true foundation of what in modern times might be called the Art of Accountancy.

To weld together into a well balanced whole the two plans of accountancy education, as embraced in the curricula of universities and colleges offering training to the embryo accountant, has long been the goal of his educational endeavors, i. e., to leaven the purely academic training by instructors or professors whose own knowledge of accountancy is in the main pedagogical, with the practical knowledge as imparted by the practicing accountant and the business man. (The author, in the American Association of Public Accountants Year Books for 1911-12-13 and 14, has gone into this subject extensively, showing that educational institutions of the country have chosen either the one or the other of the two methods of teaching—the academic training in pure theory, treated in much the same manner as economic subjects are presented and without the same degree of accuracy, or the practical lecturing upon accountancy subjects by practicing accountants and business men, supplemented by the best text books obtainable—and urging the while the necessity for the development together of the two accountancy educational plans, as is done in Great Britain.)

While it is true that to men of little or no practical experience in accountancy must be given the credit for producing some of the finest examples of purely theoretical accounting which the literature of accountancy has today, the first mentioned criticism that this pedagogical instruction does not teach the actual application of the theory to modern business, again applies. On the other hand, with the practical accountant as the instructor or the writer of text books, too little cannot be said of the difficulty he has in imparting to students and laymen the principles which see exceedingly clear to him. And it was through this research, this labor to combine in accountancy education theory with practice and practice with theory, that this book was born. It is apparent in reading the ancient works of Pacioli, of Stevin and Pietra, in their exhaustive explanations and their lengthy and precise instructions that in their endeavors to systematize the recording of the transactions of commerce of their time, they encountered many of the same sort of, if not the identical, problems with which we are confronted today. The modern translations of their works, with the author's own views presented as notes, it is believed will shed some light into the darkness which has so long shrouded the actual foundation of the practice and the theory of the profession of public accountancy.

Denver, Colorado,
August 1914.

Made in the USA
Lexington, KY
21 February 2017